The Economic Effects of Public Stockholding Policies for Rice in Asia

This work is published under the responsibility of the Secretary-General of the OECD. The opinions expressed and arguments employed herein do not necessarily reflect the official views of OECD member countries.

This document, as well as any data and any map included herein, are without prejudice to the status of or sovereignty over any territory, to the delimitation of international frontiers and boundaries and to the name of any territory, city or area.

Please cite this publication as:
OECD (2018), *The Economic Effects of Public Stockholding Policies for Rice in Asia*, OECD Publishing, Paris.
https://doi.org/10.1787/9789264305366-en

ISBN 978-92-64-30535-9 (print)
ISBN 978-92-64-30536-6 (pdf)

Photo credits: © Stephanie Coic.

Corrigenda to OECD publications may be found on line at: *www.oecd.org/publishing/corrigenda*.
© OECD 2018

Acknowledgements

Annelies Deuss, of the OECD Directorate for Trade and Agriculture, is the lead author of this report. Chapters 2 and 3 were co-authored with Marcel Adenäuer (OECD). Research assistance was provided by Margaux Sauvaget for Chapter 1 and Armelle Elasri (OECD) for Chapter 2. Michèle Patterson provided publication support and Stephanie Coic designed the cover and schematics.

Valuable comments from OECD colleagues were greatly appreciated, including those from Jonathan Brooks, Carmel Cahill, Jared Greenville, Andrzej Kwieciński, Hubertus Gay, Kelsey Burns, Silvia Sorescu, and Gen Furuhashi.

The report also benefited from valuable inputs from the delegates to the OECD Working Party on Agricultural Policies and Markets and from comments provided by Shirley Mustafa (FAO), Wonsup Yoon, Hiroshi Akai, and members of the AMIS Global Food Market Information Group.

Table of contents

Tables

Figures

Follow OECD Publications on:

Abbreviations

AAY	Antyodaya Anna Yojana (poorest household category in India)
AMIS	Agricultural Market Information System
aT	Korea Agro-Fisheries and Food Trade Corporation
BAAC	Bank for Agriculture and Agricultural Cooperatives
BULOG	Badan Urusan Logisitk (Bureau of Logistics)
CGE	Computable General Equilibrium
CIP	Central Issue Price
COFCO	China National Cereals, Oils and Foodstuffs Corporation
DGF	Director General of Food
ERS	Economic Research Service
FAO	Food and Agriculture Organization of the United Nations
FAPRI	Food and Agriculture Policy Research Institute
FCI	Food Corporation of India
FFW	Food For Work
FOBB	Farmers Option to Buy-Back
FPMU	Food Planning Monitoring Unit
GAIN	Global Agriculture Information Network
GKP	Gabah Kering Panen (Prices for wet paddy)
GOJ	Government of Japan
HPP	Harga Pembelian Pemerintah (Government Purchasing Price)
kt	Thousand tonnes
MA	Minimum Access
MAFF	Ministry of Agriculture, Forestry and Fisheries (Japan)
MAFRA	Ministry of Agriculture, Food and Rural Affairs (Korea)
MAV	Minimum Access Volume
MFN	Most Favoured Nation
MIP	Minimum Issue Price
MMA	Minimum Market Access
MSP	Minimum Support Price
MY	Marketing Year
NFA	National Food Authority
NFSA	National Food Security Act
OMA	Ordinary Minimum Access

OMS	Open Market Sale
OMSS	Open Market Sales Scheme
OWS	Other Welfare Schemes
PDS	Public Distribution System
PFDS	Public Food Distribution System
PRSP	Public Rice Stockholding Programme
PSSE	Public Storage System for Emergencies
PWO	Public Warehouse Organization
RMR	Regular Milled Rice
SAG	State Administration of Grain
SBS	Simultaneous Buy and Sell
SINOGRAIN	China Grain Reserve Corporation
TPDS	Targeted Public Distribution System
TRQ	Tariff Rate Quota
USDA	United States Department of Agriculture
UT	Union Territory
VGD	Vulnerable Group Development
VGF	Vulnerable Group Feeding
WMR	Well Milled Rice
WTO	World Trade Organisation

ISO Currency codes

BDT	Bangladeshi Taka
BHT	Thai Bhat
IDR	Indian Rupee
INR	Indonesian Rupee
KRW	Korean Wong
JPY	Japanese Yen
PHP	Philippines Peso
RMB	Yuan Remimbi (People's Republic of China)
USD	United States Dollars

Executive summary

Public stockholding programmes, whereby governments purchase, stockpile and distribute food staples, have regained popularity as a policy tool since the 2007-08 food price crisis. Governments deploy these programmes with a view to shielding consumers from food price spikes and providing more stable domestic prices for both consumers and producers. However, these programmes may also have additional and unintentional impacts on domestic and international markets, depending on how they function and the scale of intervention.

This report focuses on the specific case of public stockholding programmes for rice in Asia and analyses how different public stockholding strategies may influence domestic and international markets over the medium term (2018 to 2030). It examines, in particular, what would happen if several countries were at the same time to either expand or reduce their levels of public rice stocks, thereby placing some bounds on the potential global impacts of these policies.

Since the impacts of these programmes differ according to how they are implemented, the report first provides an in-depth review of the functioning of public stockholding programmes in eight Asian countries (Bangladesh, the People's Republic of China, India, Indonesia, Japan, Korea, the Philippines, and Thailand). To allow comparisons across countries and facilitate the economic modelling of stockholding programmes, the report distinguishes three distinct ways in which countries can procure rice for public stocks and three distinct ways in which they can release those stocks. Specifically, governments may *procure* rice for stockholding programmes from: (1) the international market at the import price; (2) the domestic market at the market price; or (3) the domestic market at a procurement price. Governments can *release* rice from their public stocks by selling rice to: (1) the international market at the export price; (2) domestic consumers at the market price; or (3) domestic consumers at a below-market subsidised price.

Using the OECD-FAO's partial equilibrium model of world agriculture, Aglink-Cosimo, the present analysis examines the market impacts over the medium term (i.e. from 2018 to 2030) if the eight abovementioned Asian countries collectively adopt either higher or lower public stocks of rice than current norms. The level of public stock norms is set at three months of national domestic rice consumption under the high-level scenario, and at two weeks under the low-level scenario. These levels are based on historic levels for public stocks of rice in these countries.

The analysis shows that while the impacts on domestic markets are projected to vary by country, there are several common trends which indicate how a collective change in public stockholding policies could influence markets in the short- and medium-term.

Main findings

- ***The effects on domestic and international markets of changing public stocks to either higher or lower levels are expected to be most pronounced during the period in which governments adjust their public stocks to new levels.***

Under the high-level scenario, procurement is assumed to increase during a three-year transition period in order to build public stocks equivalent to three months of domestic consumption. This will reduce availability on domestic and international markets, and lead to higher domestic and international rice prices. Conversely, under the low-level scenario, domestic and international rice prices would be relatively lower in the short term as destocking would increase rice availability on the market.

- ***However, changes to public stockholding policies could also have structural impacts on domestic and international markets that persist over the medium term.***

Although the effects are more pronounced during the initial three years, the analysis shows a persistent impact over the medium term on overall procurement patterns, domestic and international prices, rice availability, private stock levels, and public expenditure. Under the high-level scenario, larger public stockholding would involve higher procurement levels, thereby raising domestic and international prices and increasing public expenditures. At the same time, rice availability would decline and private stocks would be reduced. Under the low-level scenario the opposite would apply: lower procurement levels, lower domestic and international rice prices, lower public expenditure, and higher private stocks and availability.

- ***If countries hold larger public stocks then the immediate effects of a global production shock would be lower. However, recovery from the shock would be slower too.***

As larger amounts of rice can be released from public stocks under the high-level scenario as compared to the low-level scenario, the immediate impacts of a sudden supply shock on prices and availability would be lower. However, rebuilding stocks to their original level would take more time under the high-level scenario, leading to a slower recovery from the shock.

Policy implications and future work

From a policy perspective, this analysis suggests that when governments consider raising or lowering the levels of their public stocks, they should carefully evaluate both the short-term impacts and the medium-term structural effects these changes might have on domestic and international markets.

A principal motivation that governments claim for keeping large public stocks is that they can act as a safeguard against sudden supply shocks. The analysis shows that maintaining higher levels of public stocks might lessen the initial impact on price and availability from a global production shock. However, the rate of recovery towards the no-shock situation is faster if countries hold small stocks than if they hold larger ones. Furthermore, keeping low levels of public stocks significantly reduces the public expenditure bill, which frees up funds that can be used for other mitigation strategies to deal with (emergency) food shortages.

Looking ahead, the framework developed for this analysis can be used to examine and model public stocks in other countries and for other commodities. With important policy variables related to public stocks now incorporated into Aglink-Cosimo, this agricultural model can be used to examine the market impacts of other scenarios whereby countries individually or collectively change specific parameters of their public stockholding policies.

Chapter 1. The functioning of public stockholding policies

This chapter begins with a brief explanation of the different ways public stockholding policies can affect domestic and international markets, and the structure of the overall report. It then describes the functioning of public stockholding programmes for rice in eight Asian countries. It identifies for each country the agencies in charge of public stocks, the main purposes for keeping public stocks, the trade restrictions in place, how rice is procured and released from public stocks, and the associated prices. It also develops a framework that generalises the process of acquisition and release by identifying three distinct ways in which countries can procure rice for public stocks, and three distinct ways in which they can release rice from public stocks.

1.1. Introduction

Governments have a long history of using stockholding policies as part of their efforts to stabilise domestic food markets. Recourse to these policies intensified following the world food crisis of 2007-08, when the governments of numerous developing countries used the management of stocks as a way of isolating their consumers from higher prices on world grain markets. However, these programmes can also, depending on how they function and their size, have additional and unintentional impacts on domestic and international markets (Box 1.1).

Stockholding policies that aim to stabilise markets internally are controversial as they can have the effect of exporting instability onto international markets. Thus the pursuit of national food security through stockholding can potentially threaten food security in other countries.

The issue of stockholding is also closely related to the rights of developing countries to employ policies that have the effect of supporting prices to farmers (there are no constraints on supplying cheap or free food specifically to the poor). Such support policies naturally place farmers in other countries at a competitive disadvantage.

The trade-offs between domestic rights and international obligations came to a head at the WTO's 2013 Bali Ministerial Conference, where stockholding was selected as a specific issue to be addressed, with a view to unlocking the stalled Doha Round of trade negotiations. No consensus was achieved at that meeting; however, a "Peace Clause" provided some latitude to developing countries, by shielding their domestic support policies from legal challenge.

WTO members agreed that the "peace clause" would remain in force until a "permanent solution" was agreed. A permanent solution to the issue of stockholding (and associated support) should in principle account for the potential interactions between domestic and international objectives.

This report helps address a key part of the puzzle by examining the extent to which alternative levels of public stocks might influence prices and availability, both domestically and internationally. It also examines their effects on incentives for private storage and implications for public finances.

More specifically, this report takes the case of public stockholding programmes for rice in eight selected Asian countries and examines their potential domestic and international market impacts over the medium term (2018-2030). Before conducting any analysis, it is crucial to understand how these programmes function as their impacts on markets differ depending on how they are implemented. Chapter 1 therefore presents an in-depth review of these programmes, describing the agencies in charge of public stocks, the main purposes for keeping public stocks, and the accompanying trade restrictions that are in place. In addition, a framework is developed that generalizes the ways in which countries can procure and distribute rice from public stocks. A main advantage of this framework is that it facilitates translating the complex functioning of these programmes into the economic model.

Chapter 2 describes the model and the data and explains how the baseline scenario is constructed. This baseline scenario assumes a business-as-usual situation whereby countries maintain the current functioning of their stockholding programmes over the projection period (2018-2030). Chapter 3 then examines what would happen to domestic and international markets if the eight selected countries collectively scale up or down their public stockholding programmes.

Box 1.1. How can public stocks affect markets?

Stockholding programmes can impact domestic and international markets in different ways. First, they can affect domestic prices. When governments procure commodities from domestic producers to build stocks, they reduce the domestic supply in the domestic markets. If the country is not fully integrated into the world market because of trade or other barriers, then the reduction in domestic supply can lead to higher domestic prices. Likewise, when governments release their stocks on the domestic market and implement policies that limit trade, the higher domestic supply can lead to lower prices domestically.

The fact that public stocks can influence domestic prices is one of the reasons why governments implement public stockholding programmes. These stocks are usually called buffer stocks and have the explicit goal to stabilise prices. In principle, governments build buffer stocks when commodity prices fall below a certain level and release them when prices rise above a specified level. In this way, buffer stocks attempt to reduce price volatility and aim to protect producers from price drops and shield consumers from price hikes.

Public stocks can also have spill-over effects in international markets and affect trade flows and international prices. Countries that are traditionally exporters but decide to use surplus production for stock building rather than for trade will reduce the amount that is available for exports. Furthermore, governments implementing buffer stock schemes sometimes decide to implement export restrictions, which lowers export volumes even more. If the reduction in global supply is sufficiently large, it can lead to increases in international prices. Likewise, governments that decide to build stocks with imports can potentially cause world prices to rise. Conversely, the release of large quantities of public stocks on the world market can depress world prices.

The potential impact on domestic prices, international prices and trade increases with the volume of public stocks that are accumulated or released. Moreover, the prices at which commodities are purchased and released also matter. If governments buy stocks at prices that are much higher than the market prices, then the effects on domestic and international price levels will be larger. Similarly, releasing excessive amounts of stocks onto domestic (or international) markets at low prices will depress domestic (or world) prices.

Besides their impact on prices and trade, public stocks can also affect production. Governments can use public stocks not only to influence prices, but also as a way to support producers. That is, by acquiring public stocks at prices that are above the prevailing market prices, governments in fact assist producers. The higher prices in turn incentivise producers to increase their output of this particular commodity. In this sense, public stock programmes operate similarly to price support programmes and can create the same market-distorting effects.

Whereas the acquisition of public stocks aims to influence the producer side of the market, the release of public stocks targets the consumer side. Public stockholding programmes are often implemented with a view to supporting consumers. This support could be by guaranteeing lower food prices, distributing food at subsidised prices or even offering food for free during emergency situations. As such, another way in which stockholding programmes affect markets is by stimulating the consumption of the commodities that are kept in public stocks.

The effects of stockholding programmes on prices, production, consumption and trade can be compounded through their impact on the government's budget and the private sector. Previous

OECD work shows that most buffer stock programmes have not been successful in reducing price volatility, which implies that allocating public funds to these programmes comes at the expense of other policies that might actually be better suited to curbing price volatility (Deuss, 2015). In fact, some buffer stock programmes have even been found to increase price volatility (World Bank, 2012).

Another way in which public stockholding programmes affect markets is by their impact on the private sector. Large and unpredictable government involvement in markets through public stocks discourages private sector investment and participation. As the private sector withdraws from storage and trading activities, fewer actors remain in the market to stabilise prices, which eventually can lead to higher price volatility.

Sources

Deuss, A. (2015), "Review of the performance and impacts of recent stockholding policies", in *Issues in Agricultural Trade Policy: Proceedings of the 2014 OECD Global Forum on Agriculture*

World Bank (2012), "Using Public Food grain Stocks to Enhance Food Security", *Report Number 71280-GLB*.

1.2. The working of public stockholding programmes for rice in Asia

This section is the result of a thorough examination of the functioning of public stockholding programmes for rice in eight Asian countries: Bangladesh, the People's Republic of China (hereafter "China"), India, Indonesia, Japan, Korea, the Philippines, and Thailand. These countries were selected because they have public stockholding programmes for rice and are individually represented in the Aglink-Cosimo model, which provides a mechanism to assess their market impacts.

A distinction is made between two types of stocks based on who actually owns the stocks. If the stock is owned by a public entity or state trading enterprise, then it is referred to as public (or official or government) stock. If the stock is owned by private actors (i.e. farmers, households or commercial traders), then the stock is referred to as private stock. The scope of the public stockholding policies in this work covers all types of stocks managed by the public sector, and is not limited to public stockholding for food security purposes as defined in item 3 of Annex 2 in the WTO "Agreement on Agriculture".

Public stockholding programmes are complex and how they work can be very different from one year to the next. Variation in domestic production, revised trade and agricultural policies, a new government or changes in macro-economic conditions can each result in minor or major adjustments in a country's public stockholding policy. Documenting all these changes in detail is beyond the scope of this report, which aims instead to present a comparative description of the functioning of these programmes up to the end of 2016 and structured around the following key questions:

- Which agencies are in charge of public stocks?
- What are the main purposes[1] for keeping public stocks of rice?
- How does the country acquire rice for its public stocks and at what prices?
- How does the country release rice from its public stocks and at what prices?
- Are there any trade restrictions in place?

In this chapter, the process of acquisition and release of rice from public stocks is generalised to a situation where countries can procure rice through three channels and can release rice through three channels. Specifically, governments can acquire rice for their public stocks from the international market or from the domestic market. Acquisition from the international market occurs at the import price, while rice can be bought in the domestic market at procurement prices or at market prices. Governments can release public stocks to consumers in the domestic market at a subsidised price or at the market price, or they can sell the rice in the international market at the export price.

Figure 1.1 provides a schematic representation of this process. This figure is adapted for each country to properly reflect its acquisition and release process.

Figure 1.1. The general functioning of public stockholding programmes

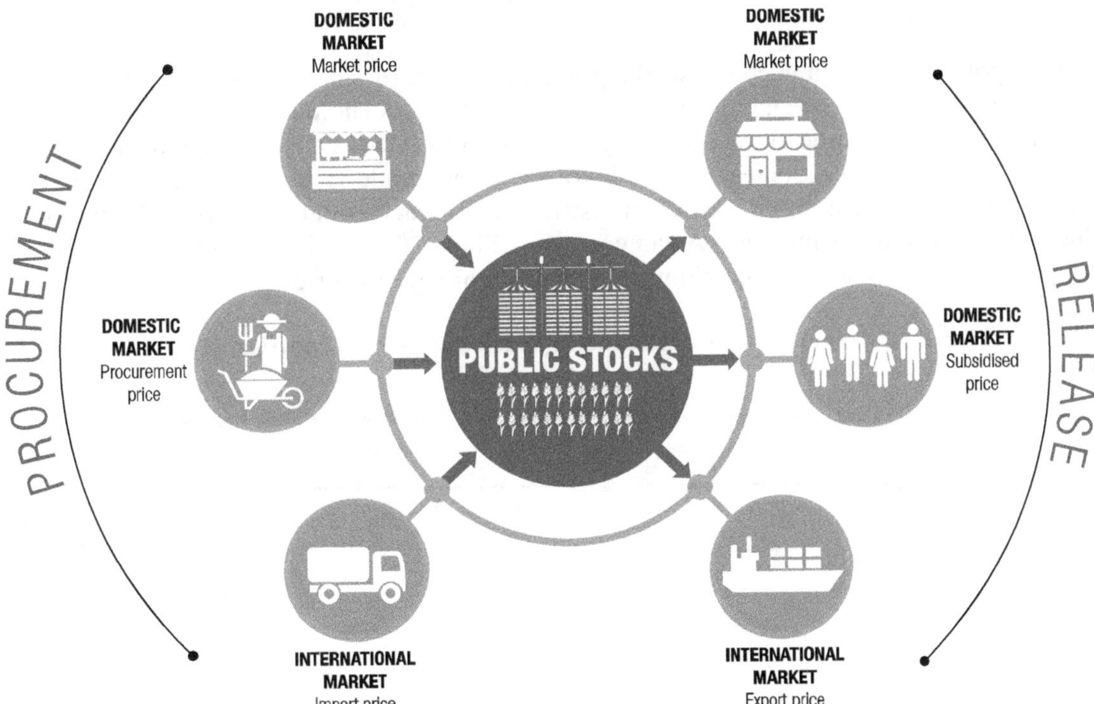

The terms procurement price, market price and subsidised price are used to indicate whether the government acquires or releases rice in the domestic market at set prices or at prevailing market prices. In particular,

- The term "procurement price" is used to indicate that the government has a mechanism in place to buy rice from farmers at a specific price and that this rice is added to the public stock. This procurement price can be above or below the farmgate price or the market price, depending on the country and the way the procurement price is calculated. In the Philippines, for example, the procurement price has, on average, been higher than the farmgate price, and Thailand set the procurement price well above the market price during its rice pledging schemes. In Indonesia, however, the government-purchasing price for wet paddy has on average been lower than the farmgate price, but much higher than the world market price.

- Procurement (release) is assumed to occur at market prices when the government buys (sells) rice in the domestic market at the prevailing prices or when the government organises auctions to buy (sell) rice for (from) its public stocks.
- The term "subsidised price" is used when the government distributes rice from its public stocks at prices below market prices or for free.

This chapter focuses on stockholding policies by considering only those situations whereby the government physically buys or releases rice from its public stocks. This implies that other types of producer support, e.g. area payments or deficiency payments, are not considered. Likewise on the consumer side, consumer support that does not include the actual distribution of rice from public stocks, for example cash transfers or food vouchers, is not described. In addition, if a country implements a price subsidy programme for consumers but there is no clear evidence that rice from public stock is explicitly used for that programme, then rice from public stocks is assumed to be distributed at market prices.

Trade policies can influence the working and objectives of stockholding programmes. A country that attempts to stabilise prices through public stockholding policies will need to be able to control trade flows. This explains why in several countries the agencies that execute stockholding policies are also involved in rice trade. This chapter therefore also describes the relevant import or export restrictions for each country. Figure 1.2 traces the net-trade positions of the eight Asian countries. Since 2011, India and Thailand are net-exporters of rice, while the remaining six countries are net-importers.

Figure 1.2. Net exports of rice in the eight selected Asian countries, 2000-2016

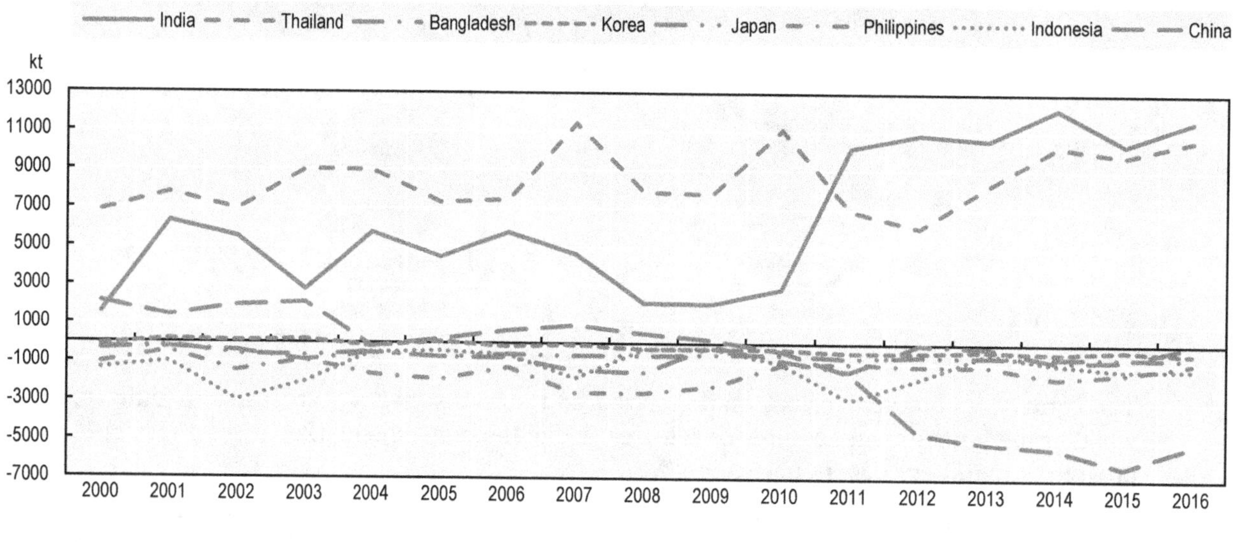

Source: OECD/FAO (2017).

Bangladesh

The main objectives of Bangladesh's public stockholding programme are to maintain grain price stability, provide grains to several social safety net programmes, and implement an effective food grain procurement scheme whereby farmers receive "fair" prices. The Directorate General of Food is in charge of the implementation of Bangladesh's national food policy strategies as well as the management and operation of the country's overall food system (Directorate General of Food, 2016).

Until 2011, the government relied on both imports and domestic procurement for its public stocks. Since 2011, public stocks have been predominantly built with domestically grown rice (GAIN-BG2001, 2012; GAIN-BG3004, 2013). The stored rice is then distributed through the Public Food Distribution System (PFDS) at subsidised prices or for free. Figure 1.3 illustrates the functioning of the public stockholding programme in Bangladesh.

The liberalisation of the food grain market in the 1990s led to increasing involvement of the private sector in rice trade and to a reduction of the public stocks (Dorosh & Childs, 2014; World Bank, 2012). This development changed when the food price crisis hit mid-2007. In response to the rising prices on the international market, Bangladesh exempted all rice from import duties in 2008, imposed an export ban on rice in May 2008[2], and started to increase its public stocks. Bangladesh lifted its export ban for aromatic rice exports in July 2012, but maintained its export ban of non-aromatic rice exports until 31 December 2015.[3] In May 2015, the country implemented a 10% import tariff on semi/wholly milled rice. This tariff was increased to 20% in December 2015, and also applied to husked and broken rice in addition to semi/wholly milled rice. In June 2016, this tariff was raised to 25% (FAO, 2016).

The large involvement of the private sector in the rice trade in the years before the food price crisis had kept domestic prices low and stable, and lowered the demand for public stocks because of the large privately-held stocks. As of 2008, Bangladesh actively expanded its public stock programme: whereas the average annual public stock levels during the period 2002/03-2006/07 were around 531 000 tonnes, this level increased to 856 000 tonnes during the period 2008/09-2013/14 (Dorosh, 2014).

Figure 1.3. Functioning of the public stockholding programme of rice in Bangladesh

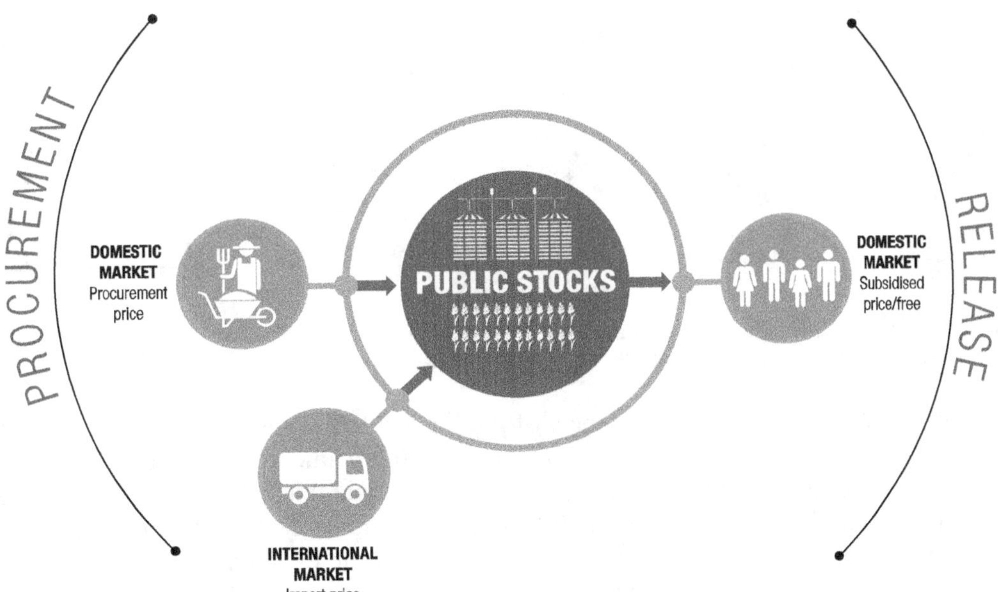

Bangladesh has three rice seasons: Boro, Aman and Aus.[4] The government procures rice predominantly during the Boro season (the largest rice crop), while the remainder is procured during the Aman season (Alam et al., 2015). Each year, a different procurement target is announced, which has ranged between 1 million and 1.5 million tonnes between 2008 and 2014, equivalent to less than 3% of production (Gain Reports for Bangladesh, several editions). The government procures paddy from farmers and milled rice from millers. The share of milled rice in total domestic procurement averaged around 80% over the last two decades (Alam et al., 2014). As a result, millers have benefited relatively more from the procurement programme than farmers have. The procurement prices for paddy and rice from the Boro and Aman season have been increasing over time. The procurement price for Boro paddy was raised from BDT 18/kg (USD 0.23[5]) in 2012 to BDT 22/kg (USD 0.28) in 2015. Over the same period, both Boro rice and Aman rice increased from BDT 28/kg (USD 0.35) to BDT 32/kg (USD 0.41) (FAO, 2016).

Rice from public stocks is released every month and distributed under the Public Food Distribution System (PFDS) through monetised channels and non-monetised (targeted) programmes (Alam et al., 2015). The share of rice distributed at subsidised prices and distributed for free varies each year. For example, in 2011 only 20% of rice was distributed through non-monetised channels, but this share increased to 80% in 2012. Figure 1.4 illustrates the amount of rice distributed through both channels between 2007 and 2012.

Figure 1.4. Distribution of rice from public stocks through monetised and non-monetised channels in Bangladesh

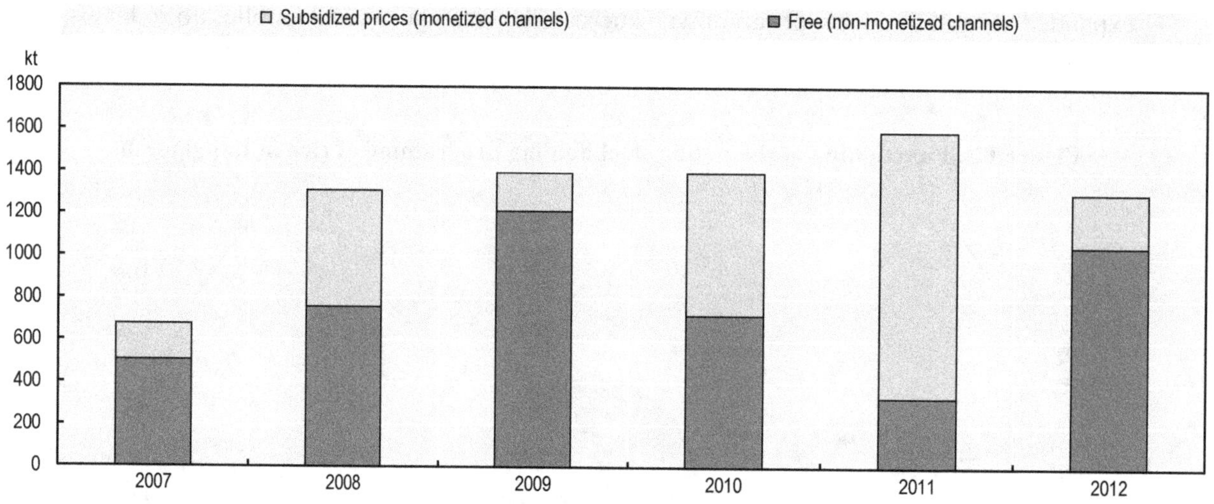

Note: Calendar years, aggregated from monthly data.
Source: Food Planning Monitoring Unit (2016).

The non-monetised distribution channels of public rice target segments of the population that cannot afford food. These channels include the Vulnerable Group Development (VGD), the Food for Work (FFW), and the Vulnerable Group Feeding (VGF) programmes. The VGD reaches 500 000 beneficiaries annually, the FFW reaches around 1 million beneficiaries, while the VGF is operational in the event of natural disasters and reaches on average 240 000 beneficiaries per year (Banerjee et al., 2014). Under the Open Market Sale (OMS) programme, individuals can purchase rice at a fixed price. In January 2010, the OMS price was BDT 24/kg (USD 0.30). This price was lowered to BDT 20/kg (USD 0.25) in November 2015 and to BDT 15/kg (USD 0.19) in February 2016 (FAO, 2016). Figure 1.5 shows that the OMS price has been lower than the average retail price of rice and the international price (Thai 5% broken) between January 2010 and June 2016.

Figure 1.5. Government-set and retail prices of rice in Bangladesh and the Thai (5% broken) export price of rice

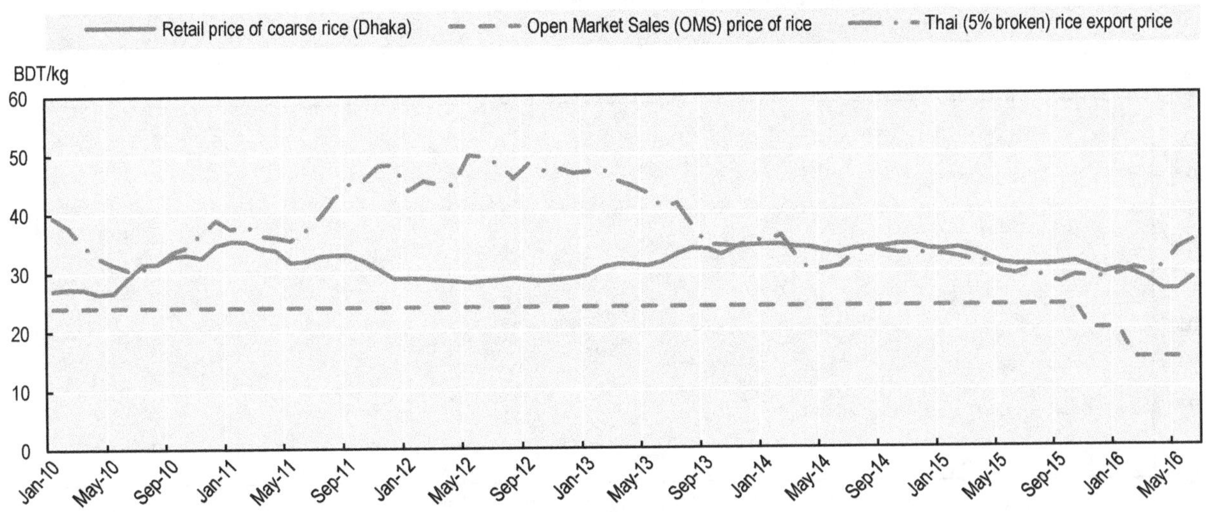

Source: Food Planning Monitoring Unit (2016) and FAO (2016).

People's Republic of China

China's public grain reserve policies are designed by the State Administration of Grain (SAG) and implemented by the China Grain Reserve Corporation, SINOGRAIN (DTB Associates, 2014). The general objective of the stockholding policy is to guarantee grain self-sufficiency. This is achieved through the promotion of domestic production, whereby SINOGRAIN procures grain from farmers at support (floor) prices. In March 2016, the support price for maize was abolished when China ended its state maize stockpiling programme, but the support prices for wheat and rice are still in place (GAIN-CH16027, 2016).

Under the price support programme for rice, which was implemented in 2004, farmers can sell their un-milled rice to SINOGRAIN when the market prices drop below the floor price. Local grain depots commissioned by SINOGRAIN are also authorized to make intervention purchases (Gale, 2013) and from 2010 onwards, the China National Cereals, Oils and Foodstuffs Corporation (COFCO) and the China Grain and Logistics Corporation were granted the same permission (DTB Associates, 2014). In order to stimulate production, the government announces the minimum prices before planting decisions are made, usually around six to nine months before the harvest (Gale, 2013). The procurement itself occurs after the harvest season; un-milled early indica rice is procured from July to September, medium and late indica rice from September to January, and japonica rice from November to February (GAIN-CH16027, 2016).

The floor prices for un-milled rice remained unchanged during the first years of the programme, but were increased annually from 2008 onwards (Figure 1.6). In 2015, however, the government decided not to increase the floor price in an attempt to reduce the widening gap between the international and domestic prices, and to slow down the accumulation of huge stockpiles of rice (OECD, 2016). This decision was extended in

2016, with floor prices for japonica and medium and late indica kept at their 2014 levels, while the floor price for early indica was 1.5% lower in 2016 compared to 2014 (GAIN-CH16027, 2016).

Figure 1.6. Procurement prices for un-milled japonica, early indica, and medium and late indica rice in China

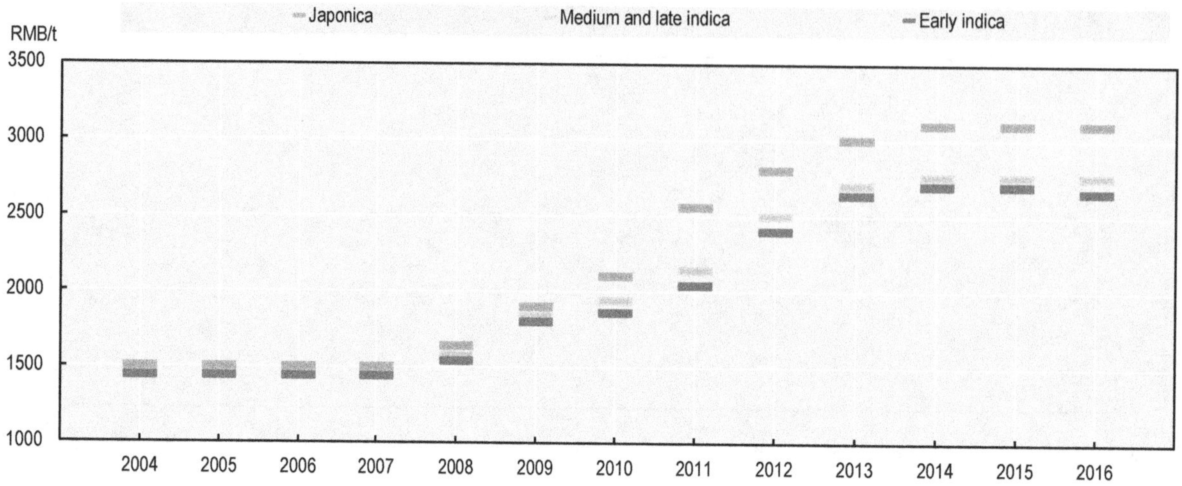

Source: Gain reports for China (several editions).

Chinese public stocks are designed to work as a buffer stock, whereby the government releases rice from its stocks when consumer prices are high or demand is large. The release of rice occurs through auctions organised by the government. A minimum auction bid is set, determined by the procurement price and storage costs (Cheng, 2011). However, these minimum auction bids are not often accepted because they are considered to be too high. As a result, the rice is not auctioned off and accumulates in the state reserves (Gale, 2013).

The support price system in combination with the sluggish release of rice from the state reserves has led to excessive public stocks of rice. The exact level of these stocks remains a state secret, and information on the volumes of procurement and distribution are also not publicly available (Carter et al., 2012). Several agencies publish estimates about Chinese total stock levels in their reports. For example, the USDA estimated that by February 2016, the Chinese government had procured 32 million tonnes of rice at minimum prices, which represents 16% of production. The ending stocks of rice for marketing year 2015/16 were estimated at 50 million tonnes (GAIN-CH16027, 2016).

Public stocks are predominantly composed of domestic rice, although they can be supplemented with rice imports (GAIN-CH15014, 2015). Interestingly, China was a net-exporter of rice for many years, but this changed in 2011 (Figure 1.8). In 2016, China's official imports amounted to 3.5 million tonnes of rice. This amount is below its tariff rate quota (TRQ) level of 5.32 million tonnes, which is associated with an in-quota tariff rate of 1%, compared with an out-of-quota tariff rate of 65%. The government controls rice imports tightly, with 50% of the TRQ reserved for state-owned enterprises (Tobias et al., 2012). In 2015, a change in China's TRQ policy was enacted to address difficulties in reducing its excessive rice stocks. In particular, importers could receive an import quota only when they had purchased grain from the state reserves (GAIN-CH15014, 2015). It is not clear whether this policy was applied in 2016.

Figure 1.7. Functioning of the public stockholding programme of rice in China

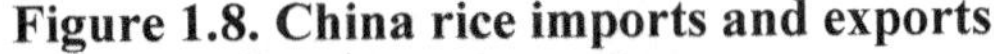

Figure 1.8. China rice imports and exports

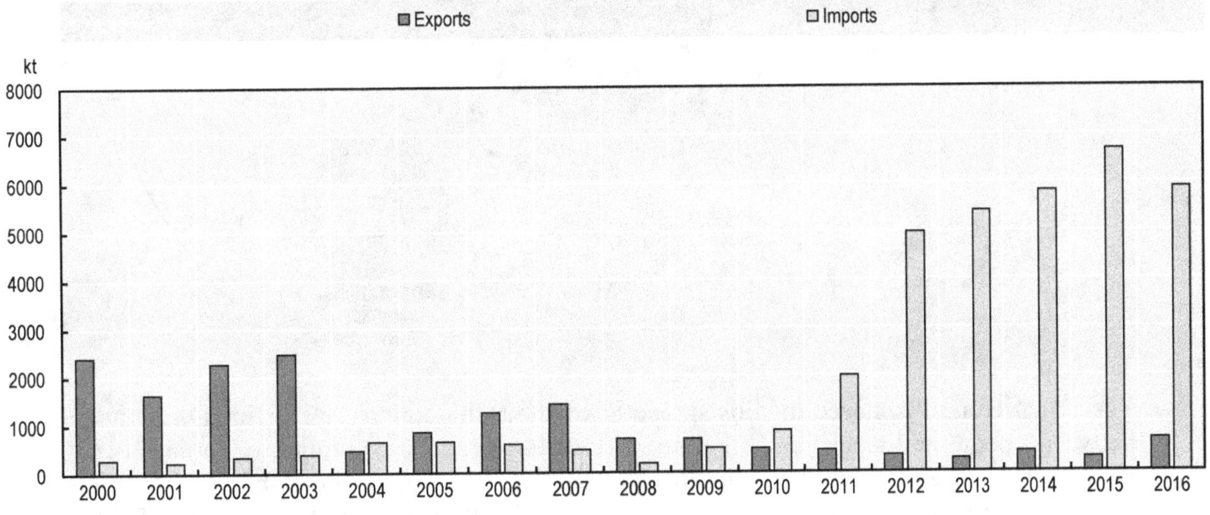

Source: OECD-FAO (2017).

India

Public stocks in India are managed by the Food Corporation of India (FCI). The stated objectives of the FCI are: i) to provide farmers remunerative prices; ii) to make food grains available at reasonable prices, particularly for vulnerable sections of society; iii) to maintain buffer stocks as a measure of food security; and iv) to intervene in the market to ensure price stabilisation (Food Corporation of India, 2016).

Figure 1.9 illustrates the functioning of the public stockholding programme in India. Before planting starts, the Minimum Support Price (MSP) is announced. The MSP is set by the Commission for Agricultural Costs and Prices and takes into consideration the cost of production and aims to offer a "reasonable margin" to farmers. After harvest, the FCI and state agencies procure paddy from the farmers at the MSP. The procurement system is open-ended since the FCI guarantees it will buy all paddies offered by farmers at the MSP, provided the grains meet certain quality specifications.

Figure 1.9. Functioning of the public stockholding programme of rice in India

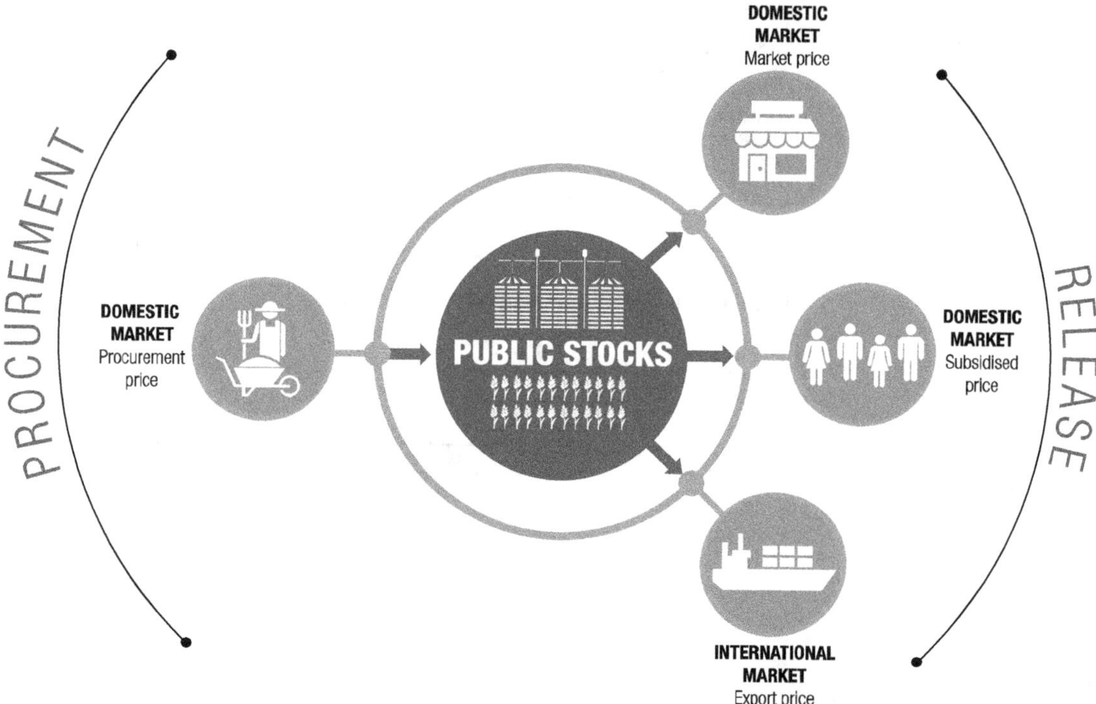

The procured rice is stored in silos spread throughout the country. A distinction is made between operational stocks and food security stocks (Food Corporation of India, 2016). Operational stocks are used for the distribution of rice through the Public Distribution System (PDS), which is comprised of the Targeted Public Distribution System (TPDS) and Other Welfare Schemes (OWS). Food security stocks are kept to meet shortfalls in procurement due, for example, to natural calamities.

The 2008 food price crisis triggered a rise in public stock levels, which almost tripled between 2007-08 and 2012-13 (Figure 1.10). Stock levels have decreased since then, but are still well above the public stocking norms set by the government. These norms indicate the minimum amount of rice that has to be maintained in the central pool at the beginning of each quarter. The norm for the operational stocks changes on a quarterly basis, with different levels prescribed on the first day of January, April, July and October, while the norm for the food security (strategic) stocks is fixed for the entire year. Procurement of rice peaked during the food price hikes of 2008 and 2011. Since 2013, India has procured each year around 30% of domestic production.

Figure 1.10. Rice production, procurement, public stock level and norm in India

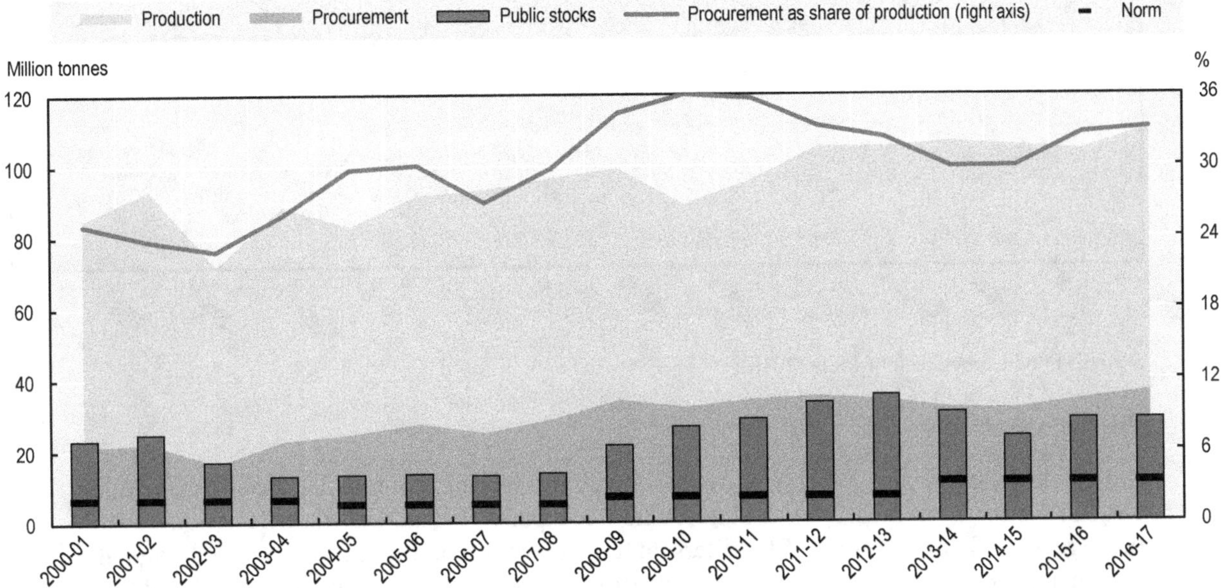

Note: All rice quantities are on a milled basis.
Source: Reserve Bank of India (2017).

The central government, through the FCI, issues the rice for the PDS to state governments at the Central Issue Price (CIP). States then distribute rice to consumers through the TPDS and OWS at subsidised prices. In 2013, India passed the National Food Security Act (NFSA) which expanded the coverage of the TPDS. Under this act, 75% of the rural population and 50% of the urban population are eligible to receive 5 kg/person/month of food grains at INR 3 (USD 0.04), INR 2 (USD 0.03) and INR 1 (USD 0.01) per kg for rice, wheat and coarse grains respectively (DFPD, 2016). The existing AAY[6] households continue to receive 35 kg of food grains per household per month. By November 2016, all 36 States and Union Territories (UT) had implemented the NFSA (Government of India, 2016).

As illustrated in Figure 1.9, rice from public stocks can be released at subsidized prices through the PDS, can be sold in the Open Market Sales Scheme (OMSS) at the Minimum Issue Price or can be exported. Figure 1.11 compares the amount of rice released by the FCI for the TPDS ("TPDS offtake") with the total amount of rice released ("total offtake"). Between 2003 and 2011, around 60% of the rice in public stocks was released through the TPDS. This share increased considerably in the following years, reaching 90% since 2012-13. The remaining rice is mostly released for the OWS. Since 2012, almost no rice from public stocks has been exported or sold in the OMSS.

Even though India restricted rice exports between 2008 and 2011 through the use of export bans, quotas and minimum export prices, it no longer restricts its rice trade. Since 2012, India is the world's largest rice exporter.

Figure 1.11. Total offtake and TPDS offtake of rice in India

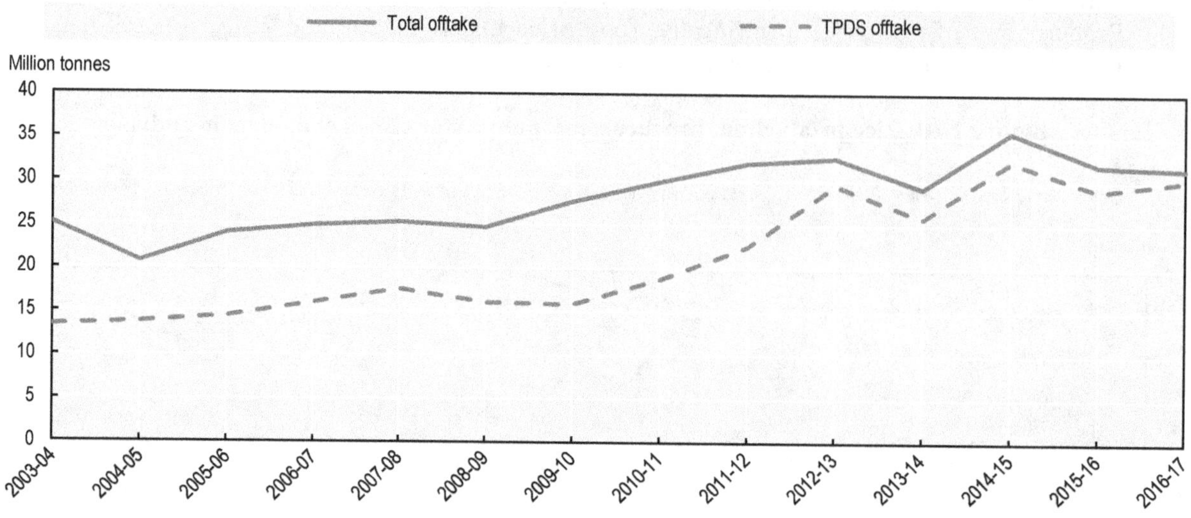

Source: Food Corporation of India (2018).

Indonesia

Indonesia's public rice reserves are administered by the Bureau of Logistics (Badan Urusan Logisitk or BULOG), a state-owned company. BULOG's main functions are to procure rice from farmers and millers at the government purchase price, manage the public rice stocks, distribute rice at subsidised prices to the poor through the Raskin programme, and release rice on the domestic market when retail prices are too high or when emergency situations arise (BULOG, 2016).

Public rice stocks are composed of domestic and imported rice. Priority is always given to domestically-produced rice, but when domestic procurement cannot fulfil the minimum stock and procurement targets, BULOG is authorised by the government to import rice. In 2013, the minimum stock level target was set at 2 million tonnes, but this level changes on a yearly basis (GAIN-ID1318, 2013).

Like many other Asian countries, the government of Indonesia complements its stockholding policies with strong restrictions on rice imports and exports. The Food Law of 2012 and Regulation 19/M-DAG/PER/3/2014 (Republic of Indonesia, 2014) cover most of the recent policy measures. The latter regulation reclassified rice and banned private imports of medium quality rice, giving BULOG a monopoly on these imports. Private imports of specialty rice and rice required for food manufacturing purposes are still permitted (GAIN-ID1412, 2014). All rice imports are restricted in time and are not allowed one month prior to, during and two months after the main harvest period. A Most Favoured Nation (MFN) import tariff of IDR 450/kg (USD 0.034) has been applied to rice since 2008 (WTO, 2016). Rice exports are heavily regulated and only allowed if domestic supply exceeds demand. Indonesia has not exported rice in recent years, due not only to its lack of excess supply of rice, but mostly because its domestic prices are much higher than international prices.

Figure 1.12. Functioning of the public stockholding programme of rice in Indonesia

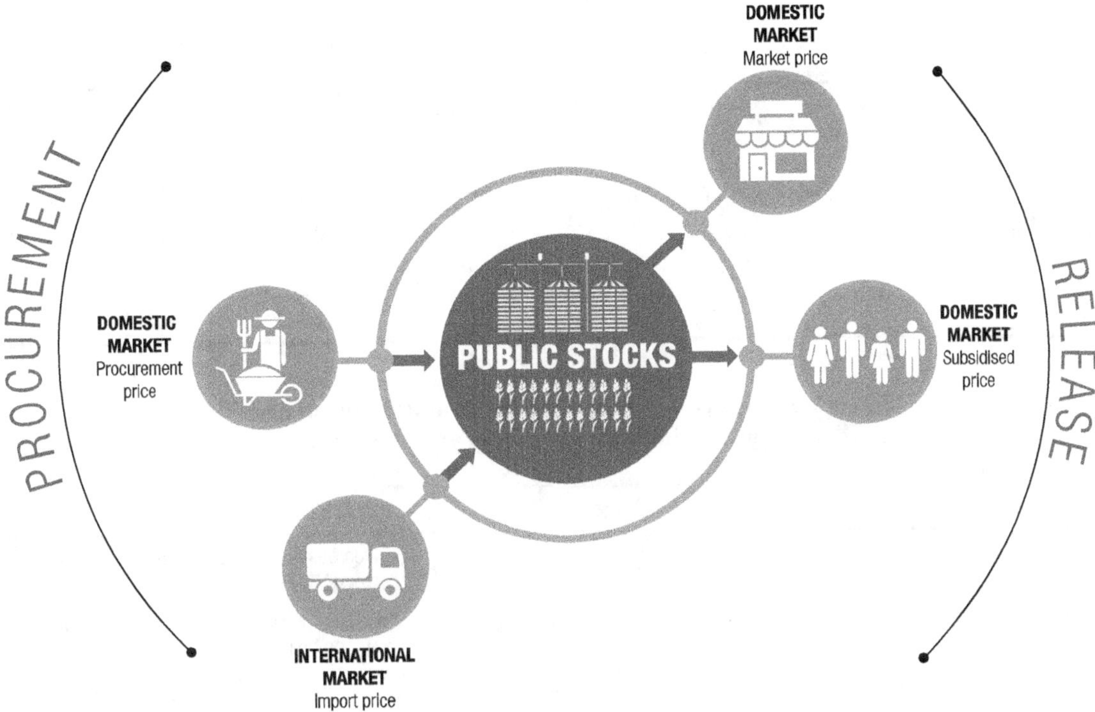

BULOG procures rice from farmers or millers at government purchasing prices, called the Harga Pembelian Pemerintah (HPP). The government sets different purchasing prices depending on the production form (wet paddy, dry paddy, or rice sold at farmgate, mill or BULOG warehouse) and the quality of the rice (Table 1.1). Since May 2008, the HPP for wet paddy at the farmgate level has been lower than the average farmgate price (Statistic Indonesia, 2016). This is illustrated in Figure 1.13.

Indonesia distributes rice from public stocks for three distinct purposes: price stabilisation, social aid, and emergencies. Table 1.2 lists the ministries in charge of each of these distribution purposes and the corresponding legislative documents. When consumer prices are 10% higher than a calculated average price[7] for at least one week, the government will consider releasing rice from its national reserve for price stabilization purposes.

Around 90% of Indonesia's public stock is distributed through the Raskin programme as social aid (Alavi and Htenas, 2014). In marketing year (MY) 2015/16, BULOG allocated 2.795 million tonnes of rice to the Raskin programme, which is equivalent to 7% of domestic demand. This rice will be distributed to more than 15.5 million poor families[8] who can buy up to 15 kg/month of rice at the subsidised price of IDR 1 600/kg (USD 0.12) (GAIN-ID1610, 2016).

**Table 1.1. Government Purchasing Price (HPP) in Indonesia,
IDR/kg, 2007-2016**

	2007	2008	2009	2010-11	2012-14	2015-16
Wet paddy (GKP) at farmer level	2 000	2 200	2 400	2 640	3 300	3 700
Wet paddy (GKP) at milling level	2 035	2 240	2 440	2 685	3 350	3 750
Dry paddy (GKG) at milling level	2 575	2 800	3 000	3 300	4 150	4 600
Dry paddy (GKG) in Bulog storage	2 600	2 840	3 040	3 345	4 200	4 650
Rice in Bulog storage	4 000	4 300	4 600	5 060	6 600	7 300
Presidential instruction	3/2007	8/2008	8/2008	7/2009	3/2012	5/2015

**Table 1.2. Government rice stock distribution in Indonesia:
Purpose, ministries in charge, and legislation**

Purpose distribution	Ministry in charge	Legal document
Price stabilisation	Ministry of Trade	Decree of Trade Ministerial No. 04/M-DAG/PER/1/2012
Social aid (Raskin)	Ministry of Welfare Coordinator	Decree of Welfare Coordinator Ministerial No. 03/2011
Emergencies (e.g. natural disasters and social conflict)	Ministry of Social Services	Decree of Social Ministerial No. 20/2012

**Figure 1.13. Average farmgate price and government purchase price for wet paddy
in Indonesia, January 2008-December 2016**

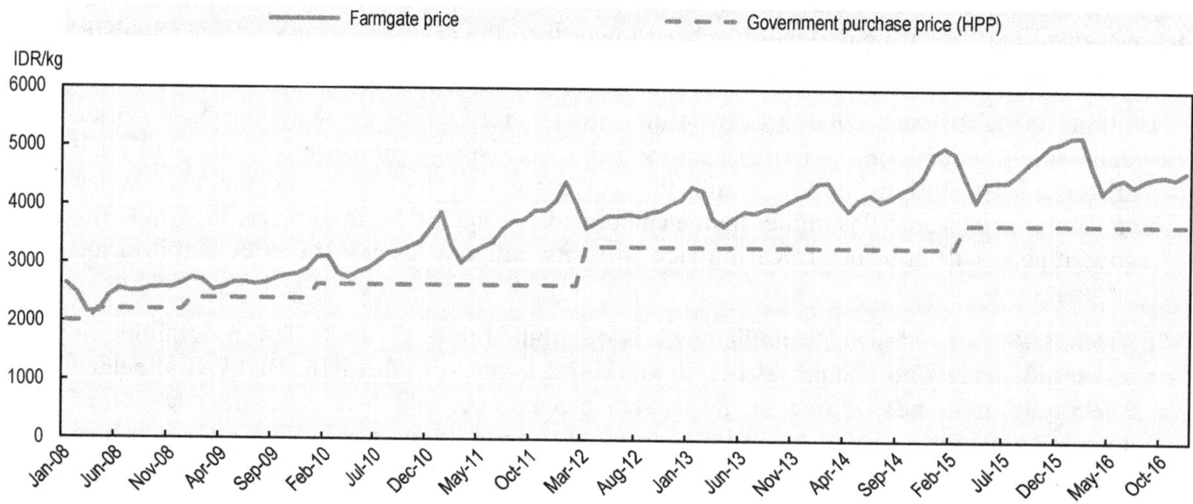

Note: Prices for wet paddy or Gabah Kering Panen (GKP).
Source: Statistic Indonesia (2016).

Japan

Japan's public stock for food security purposes is composed of domestic rice. This reserve stock, called the Government of Japan (GOJ) stock, is managed by the Ministry of Agriculture, Forestry and Fisheries (MAFF). In addition to the GOJ stock, MAFF also stores rice imported through state trading enterprises under its minimum access commitment. This second type of public stock, composed of Ordinary Minimum Access (OMA) rice, is a working stock for commercial purposes and is unrelated to Japan's food security programme. Figure 1.14 illustrates the overall functioning of the two stocks and Table 1.3 presents the levels of those stocks between 2006 and 2015.

The GOJ stockholding programme was significantly reformed in 2011. Before the reform, rice for the GOJ stock was bought after harvest (around December), the amount of rice that was acquired varied each year and the stored rice was sold as food. Since 2011, rice for the GOJ stock is contracted in fixed amounts (of around 200 000 tonnes per year, which is equivalent to 2% of total rice production) before the planting (around April) and is mainly sold as feed. The government abolished the administered price for rice in 2004 (OECD, 2009) and as a result, rice for GOJ stocks is procured from domestic producers through auctions at prices that are close to the domestic market price, but are much higher than the international reference price (e.g. the Thai export fob price of rice). These changes are in line with the new purpose of the programme, where public stocks are held predominantly to guarantee food security in times of unstable supply and should not affect domestic supply, demand and prices (MAFF, 2016b).

Figure 1.14. Functioning of the public stockholding programme of rice in Japan

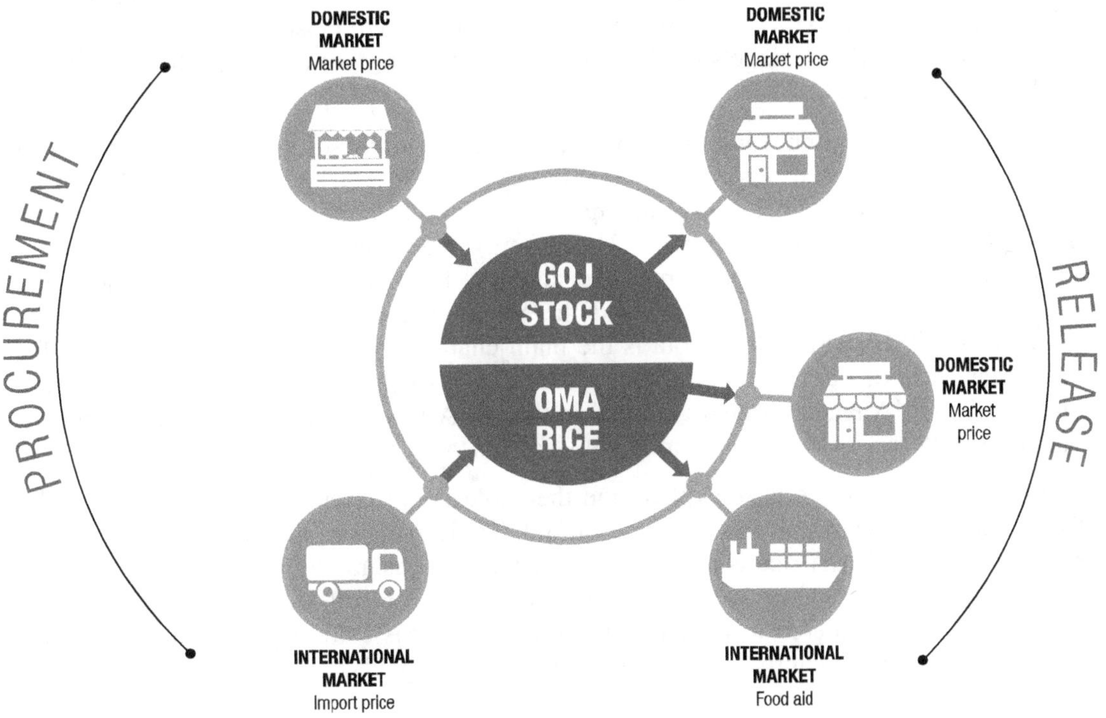

Note: GOJ stands for Government of Japan; OMA stands for Ordinary Minimum Access.

**Table 1.3. Government of Japan (GOJ) and Ordinary Minimum Access (OMA) stock levels
(1 000 tonnes, brown rice basis)**

	GOJ reserve stock (domestic rice)	OMA working stock (imported rice)
2006	770	1 890
2007	770	1 520
2008	990	970
2009	860	950
2010	980	880
2011	880	960
2012	950	780
2013	910	800
2014	910	840
2015	910	730

Note: Carry-over stock data. Data for GOJ stock refer to the crop year July-June (i.e. 2014: July 2014 – June 2015). Data for OMA rice refer to the period November-October (i.e. 2014: November 2014 – October 2015). These classifications are consistent with Aglink-Cosimo. However, note that in MAFF documents, OMA rice for 2014 refer to November 2013-October 2014.
Source: MAFF (2016a), GAIN-JA5009 (2015) and GAIN-JA6004 (2016).

Rice from the GOJ stock will be sold as table rice only in cases when an emergency situation arises. To determine whether the country faces an emergency situation, MAFF has designed a three-step process which is composed of a regular survey, an urgent survey and a Food Section Meeting. In the absence of an emergency situation, the rice will be stored for a maximum of five years, after which it will be sold mostly for feed use. This implies that MAFF targets holding around 1 million tonnes of rice in the GOJ stocks (Tobias et al., 2012).

Japan uses a TRQ system for its rice imports. In-quota purchases are under the control of the government and the out-of-quota tariff is set at JPY 341/kg (USD 2.97). Under its Minimum Access (MA) commitment, Japan is required to import at least 682 200 tonnes of rice (milled basis), equivalent to 7.2% of its average domestic consumption between 1986 and 1988. These imports enter the country through two different channels: the Ordinary Minimum Access (OMA) and the Simultaneous Buy and Sell (SBS) tender system. The OMA part of the quota is the main channel for rice imports, accounting for more than 90% of rice imports between 2013 and 2015 (MAFF, 2016b). Rice imported through the OMA tender system is stored in the OMA working stocks, and rice imported under the SBS tender system is immediately sold as table rice.

The OMA imported rice is stockpiled and then sold for different uses: as an input in the food processing sector, as feed, or as food aid. Table 1.4 gives an overview of the MA rice sales by use. OMA rice is mainly used for feed. Prices at which rice is sold are close to market prices since they occur through auctions. As a result, the selling of OMA rice for feed use is considered to be a fiscal burden since it is sold at prices similar to corn feed, which are significantly lower than the import price paid.

**Table 1.4. Minimum Access rice sales by use in Japan
(1 000 tonnes, brown rice basis)**

	Table rice (SBS)	Processing (OMA)	Feed (OMA)	Food aid (OMA)
2006	100	250	150	130
2007	110	360	580	80
2008	100	370	660	120
2009	80	210	250	200
2010	80	210	420	140
2011	10	150	380	90
2012	80	150	450	190
2013	100	190	330	100
2014	40	150	440	40
2015	10	110	650	60

Note: The Japanese marketing year runs from November to October, hence values under 2014 refer to the period November 2013 until October 2014.
Source: MAFF (2016a, 2016b, 2016c), GAIN-JA5009 (2015) and GAIN-JA6004 (2016).

Korea

Korea's Public Rice Stockholding Programme (PRSP) was established in 2005. The PRSP is under the responsibility of the Ministry of Agriculture, Food and Rural Affairs (MAFRA). Contrary to the previous programme, whereby farmers received support prices, the current programme purchases rice from farmers at the market price during the harvest season (October to December). The stocked rice is then released during the non-harvest months at prevailing market prices (OECD, 2016). Under Article 9 of the Grain Management Act, the rice can be sold for different uses, including governmental, processing, public and private uses (Grain Management Act, 2016). The main purposes of the programme are to guarantee food security in times of emergencies (e.g. natural disasters) or when there is a temporary grain shortage due to unstable supply and demand. Because of its latter purpose, the programme is also known as the Public Storage System for Emergencies (PSSE). The level of rice stock is targeted at around 17% of total consumption.

In addition to the public stocks that consist of domestically produced rice, Korea also holds a second type of public stocks which are entirely composed of imported rice (GAIN-KS1613, 2016). These stocks are held separately from the domestic rice stocks (Figure 1.15). Figure 1.16 shows the amount of domestic and imported rice kept in public stocks annually over the period 2005-2013.

On 1 January 2015, Korea replaced its non-tariff barriers by a tariff-based system. As a result, Korea applies a tariff rate of 513% on rice imports and maintains a TRQ of 408 700 tonnes with a duty level of 5%. TRQ table rice is managed by the Korea Agro-Fisheries and Food Trade Corporation (aT), while TRQ rice for processing purposes is imported by MAFRA and managed by local governments. The aT sells table rice through auctions, whereas processing rice is sold at a set price (GAIN-KS1613, 2016). MAFRA exclusively controls the country's rice imports (WTO, 2014; Grain Management Act, 2016).

Figure 1.15. Functioning of the public stockholding programme of rice in Korea

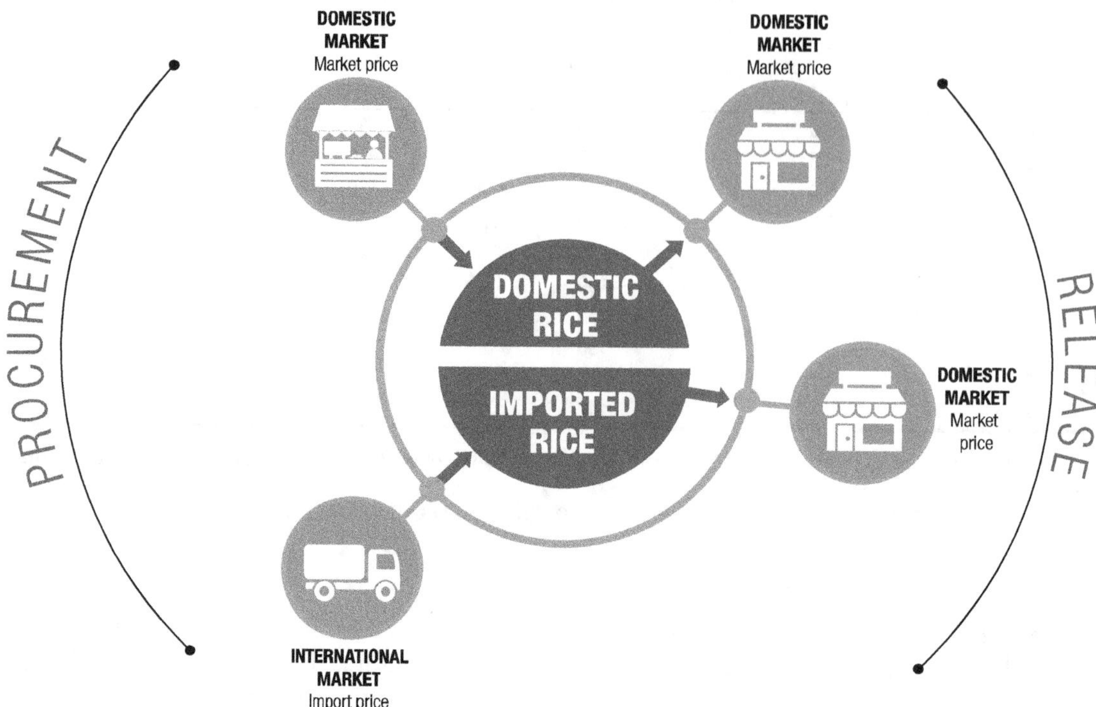

Figure 1.16. Composition of public stocks of milled rice in Korea

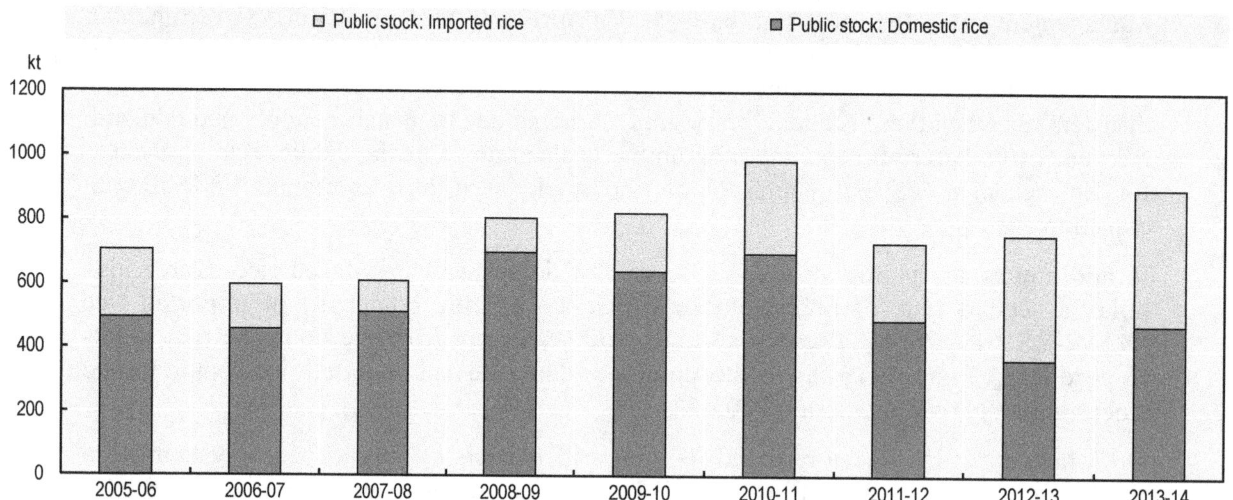

Note: The Korean rice year runs from November to October. Stock levels of milled rice at end of October.
Source: Gain Reports for Korea (several editions).

The PRSP purchases rice during the harvest period from rice farmers. Purchase quantities for public stockholding are determined through a cabinet meeting presided by the president and the result is announced to the public. In 2014 and 2015, public stock purchases from domestic farmers amounted to 370 000 tonnes and 360 000 tonnes (MAFRA notifications 2014-261 and 2015-133), which represented around 8.7% and 8.3% of domestic production, respectively (Figure 1.17).

Figure 1.17. Government domestic rice purchases in Korea

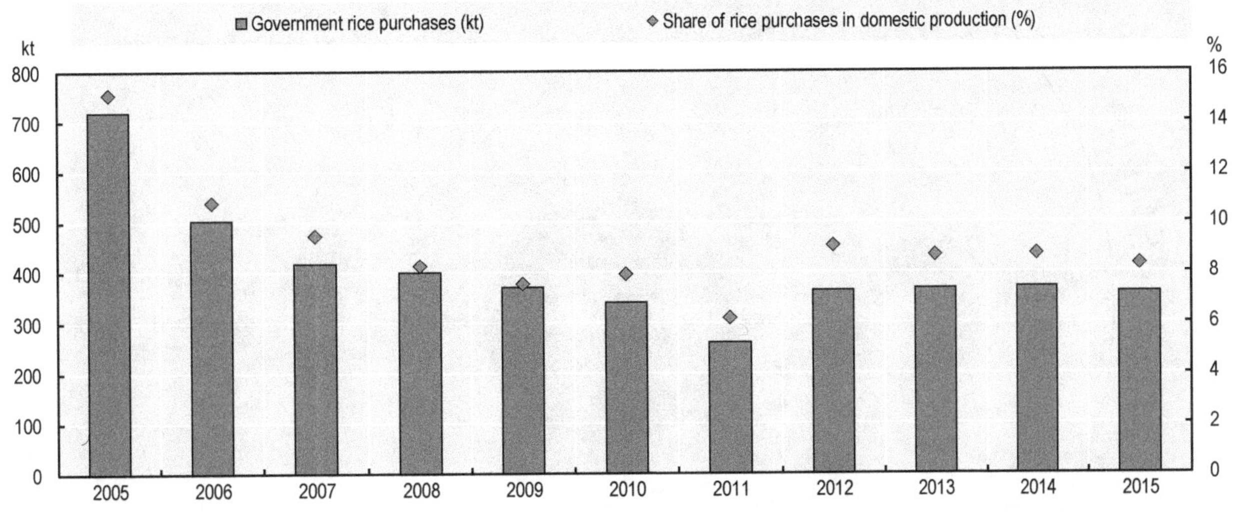

Source: GAIN-KS1613 (2016).

Philippines

In the Philippines, the government-owned National Food Authority (NFA) is in charge of the country's public stockholding programme. Its mandate is to "ensure national food security and stabilise supply and prices of staple cereals both in the farm and consumer levels" (NFA, 2016a). In addition to managing the government's rice stockholding programme, the NFA also enjoys supplementary powers such as control of rice imports, exports, and post-harvest facilities (Briones & dela Pena, 2015).

The Philippines is a net-importer of rice with strong government involvement. In July 2014, the country received approval from the WTO Council for Trade in Goods to extend its special treatment of rice until 30 July 2017, provided that it relaxed its import restrictions. As a result, the country lowered its in-quota tariffs from 40% to 35% and increased the annual Minimum Access Volume (MAV) from 350 000 tonnes to 805 200 tonnes. The out-of-quota tariff remained unchanged at 50% (OECD, 2017). Private traders are allowed to import rice under the MAV programme through permits and allocations granted to them by the NFA via auctions.

Figure 1.18 illustrates the general functioning of the public stockholding programme in the Philippines. The NFA procures paddy during harvest times from farmers and farmers' organizations at support prices, stocks this acquired paddy, outsources the milling of the paddy, and then distributes the milled rice through different channels to consumers at subsidised prices (NFA, 2016a). At times of rice shortages, the NFA will import rice to guarantee the stability of rice supplies and prices.

The NFA is mandated to maintain at least 15 days of overall national rice consumption in stock at all times for food security purposes. This amount increases to 30 days during the lean months (July-September). In December 2015, 15 days of rice stock were equivalent to 482 386 tonnes (NFA, 2015). In order to maintain at least 99% of its stock fit for human consumption, the NFA stores rice for at most six months and paddy rice for at most nine months (Commission on Audit, 2015). Total stocks, namely those held by the government, households and private warehouses, should be equivalent to 90 days of consumption (SEPO, 2010).

Figure 1.18. Functioning of the public stockholding programme of rice in the Philippines

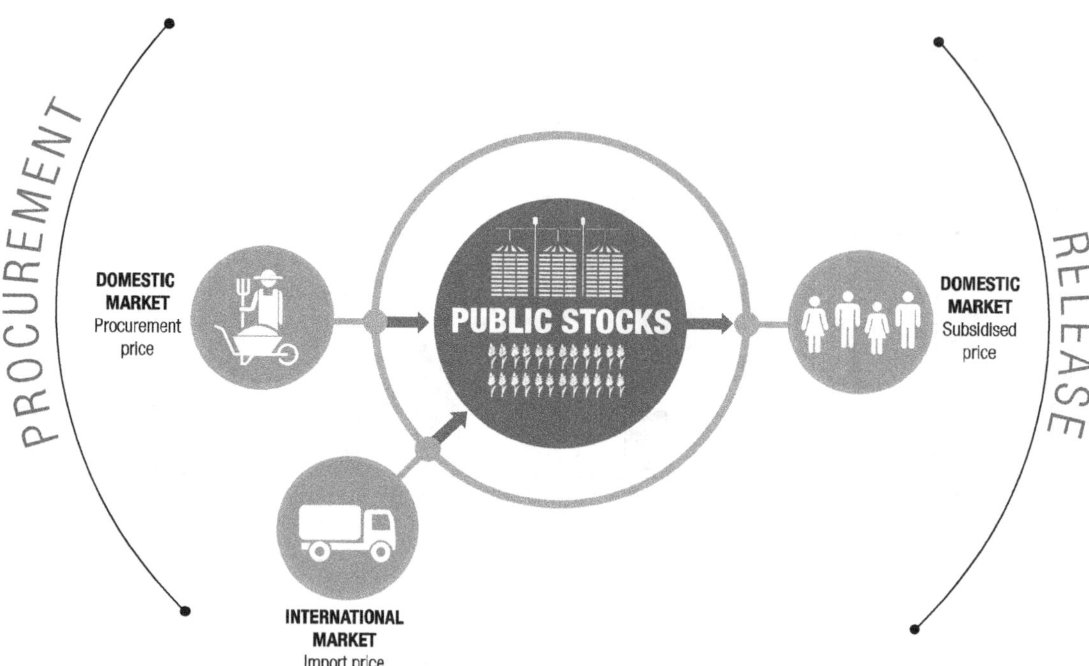

The NFA builds its stocks with rice procured from the domestic market at a support price (NFA buying price) and with imports. In general, the stocks are mostly composed of imported rice. Paddy procured from the domestic market usually represents less than 5% of production (Figure 1.19). The government sets a target of how much it will procure from the market each year; however, there does not appear to be any consistent threshold level for paddy procurement (Briones & dela Palma, 2015).

The support price is administratively set based on the average domestic cost of production plus a determined mark-up (OECD, 2017). Table 1.5 compares the support price with the average farmgate price during the period 2000-2015. The support price was raised twice during the last 15 years and in most years the support price was on average higher than the farmgate price. When the market prices are higher than the NFA support price, farmers can make use of the Farmers Option to Buy Back (FOBB) Programme. Under this programme, farmers have the option to buy back within six months the same volume of stocks they sold to NFA and sell it to traders at the prevailing market price (NFA, 2015).

The NFA sells milled rice under its distribution programme through three different types of market outlets: accredited retailers, government agencies, and private institutions. The NFA sets selling prices which differ by the type of rice and the market outlet.[9] NFA rice can be purchased by anyone and is hence a universal consumer price subsidy (Fernandez & Velarde, 2012). Table 1.5 compares the average annual NFA selling retail price with the average annual market retail price for well milled rice and regular milled rice. In the last three years, the difference between subsidised and market prices has been such that consumers who bought NFA rice saved around PHP 10/kg (USD 0.2) compared to the commercial retail rice. However, the subsidised selling price is considerably higher than the world market price (OECD, 2017).

Figure 1.19. Domestic paddy procurement, rice imports and share of domestic procurement in total domestic production in the Philippines

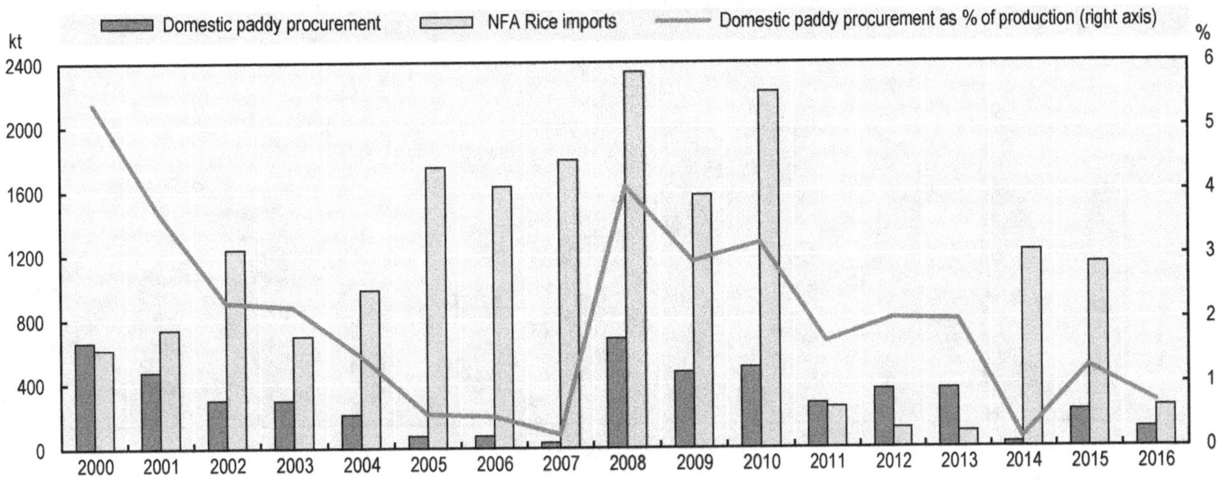

Source: Domestic paddy procurement and NFA rice imports (NFA 2013, 2014, 2015, 2016b, 2016c, 2016e), domestic paddy production (CountrySTAT Philippines, 2017a).

Table 1.5. NFA buying and selling prices, farmgate prices and retail prices of rice, 2000-2015 (PHP/kg)

	(1) NFA buying price	(2) Average farmgate price	(1)-(2)	(3) NFA selling retail price, WMR	(4) Average prevailing retail price, WMR	(4)-(3)	(5) NFA selling retail price, RMR	(6) Average prevailing retail price, RMR	(6)-(5)
2000	10	8.42	1.58	15	19.45	4.45	14	17.59	3.59
2001	10	8.17	1.83	18	19.43	1.43	16	17.54	1.54
2002	10	8.82	1.18	18	19.98	1.98	16	18.00	2.00
2003	10	8.84	1.16	18	20.20	2.20	16	17.95	1.95
2004	10	9.45	0.55	18	21.04	3.04	16	18.71	2.71
2005	10	10.43	-0.43	18.5	22.88	4.38	16	20.73	4.73
2006	10	10.46	-0.46	18	23.56	5.56	16	21.28	5.28
2007	11	11.22	-0.22	18	24.72	6.72	16	22.39	6.39
2008	17	14.13	2.87	30	32.71	2.71	25	29.38	4.38
2009	17	14.63	2.37	30	34.12	4.12	25	30.69	5.69
2010	17	14.87	2.13	28	34.34	6.34	25	30.84	5.84
2011	17	15.17	1.83	28	34.73	6.73	27	31.31	4.31
2012	17	16.22	0.78	28	35.30	7.30	27	32.08	5.08
2013	17	16.93	0.07	32	36.87	4.87	27	33.70	6.70
2014	17	20.07	-3.07	32	42.32	10.32	27	38.93	11.93
2015	17	17.33	-0.33	32	42.04	10.04	27	37.06	10.06
2016	17	17.43	-0.43	32	41.72	9.72	27	36.67	9.67

Note: WMR stands for well milled rice; RMR stands for regular milled rice.
Source: NFA prices 2000-2014 (Briones & dela Palma, 2015); NFA prices 2015 (NFA, 2015); NFA prices 2016 (NFA, 2016e); average farmgate prices and prevailing retail prices (CountrySTAT Philippines, 2017b and 2017c).

Figure 1.20. NFA distribution of rice in the Philippines

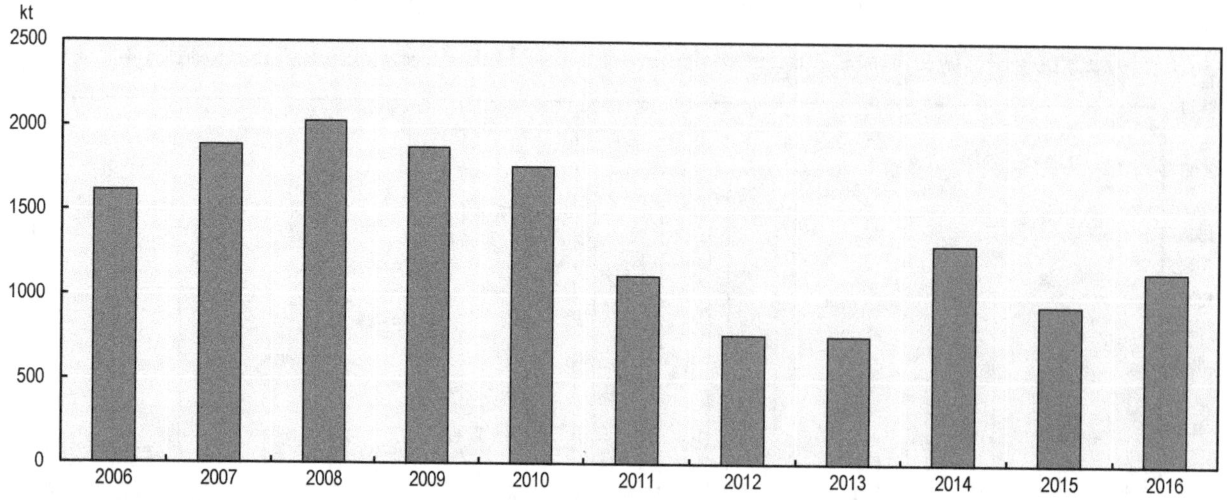

Source: NFA (2014, 2015, 2016e).

Thailand

Thailand has been one of the world's largest net exporters of rice for several decades. Accordingly, its public stockholding policies have been focused on guaranteeing an adequate income to rice farmers by providing intervention prices for their crops. Rice from the intervention stocks is mainly sold on the international market, but the government will also release rice on the domestic markets.

Thailand's public stockholding policies have undergone significant changes since 2000. To understand the evolution of its intervention stocks and prices, it is useful to make a distinction between four periods (Table 1.6).

In 2001, the Thai government implemented a national Paddy Pledging Programme which allowed farmers to choose whether to sell their rice on the market at market prices or to the government at intervention prices. Farmers who decided to sell to the government were given a loan by the Bank for Agriculture and Agricultural Cooperatives (BAAC) which was equivalent to the amount of rice they wanted to pledge times the intervention price. The maximum payment per household was set at BHT 350 000. Farmers then had four to six months to redeem the paddy (i.e. to pay the government back) or to transfer the pledged amount of paddy to the government. In the latter case, rice was stored either by the farmers themselves, who received an additional payment for this, or in one of the storage facilities managed by the Public Warehouse Organization (PWO). At the start of the programme in 2001, the government targeted the purchase of 8.7 million tonnes of rice at intervention prices which were 30% above the prevailing market price (Poapongsakorn and Charupong, 2010).

In October 2009, the Rice Pledging Programme was replaced by a Price Insurance Scheme. Instead of acquiring rice from farmers at a support price, the government provided direct payments to the farmers. These direct payments were calculated as the difference between the insured price (a set price based on the average cost of production and allowing for a profit margin of 30% to 40%) and the benchmark price (a weighted average of wholesale market prices). Under the Price Insurance Scheme, no rice was acquired by the government (GAIN-TH9161, 2009). However, the government did still purchase some rice during this period under the Direct Purchase Programme, which was implemented to stabilise domestic prices (GAIN-TH1035, 2011).

Figure 1.21. Functioning of the public stockholding programme of rice in Thailand up to 2014

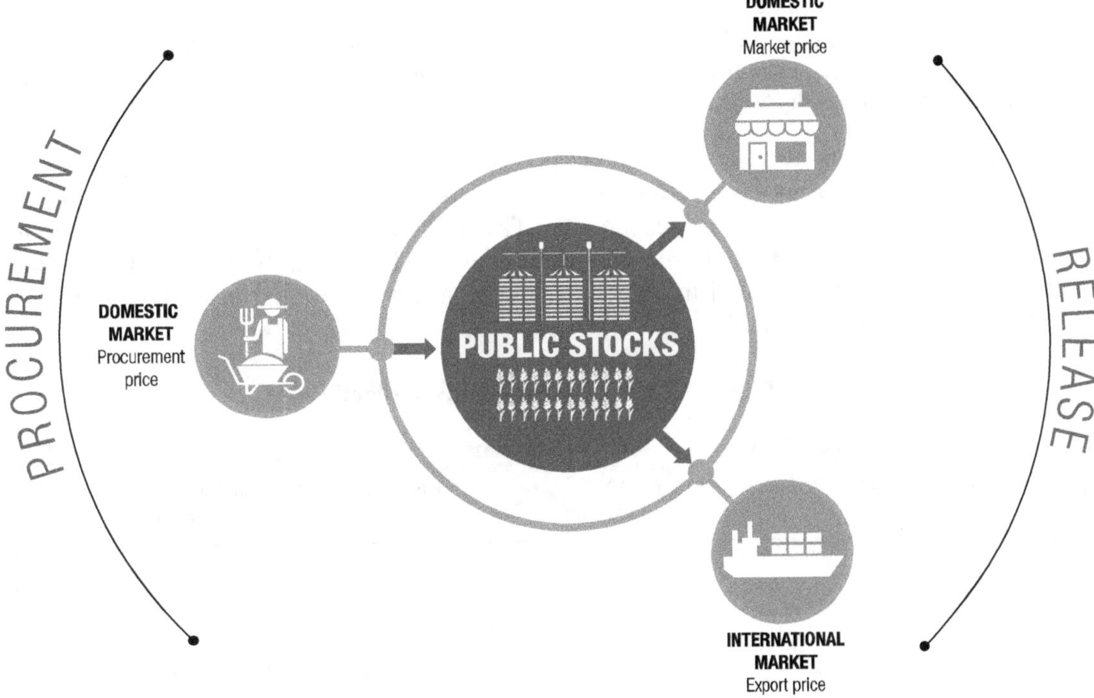

Table 1.6. Thai government rice purchasing programmes (2001 to present)

Period	Years	Name of programme	Varieties of rice purchased
Period 1	2001-2009	Paddy Pledging Programme	White, fragrant, glutinous
Period 2	2009-2011	Direct Purchase Programme	White, fragrant, glutinous
Period 3	2011-2014	Paddy Pledging Programme	White, fragrant, glutinous
Period 4	2014-now	Farmer loans to delay sales of rice paddy	Fragrant, glutinous

The Paddy Pledging Programme was re-established in October 2011. The main differences with the previous pledging programme were that the government did not impose a limit on the amount of rice that farmers could pledge and that intervention prices for both white and fragrant rice were set at 50% above the market price (GAIN-TH5030, 2015). The main purpose of the programme was to raise farmers' incomes. At the same time, the government also reduced its rice exports in an attempt to raise global prices and then sell its stocked rice at a profit. These profits would then be used to recover the costs incurred by setting a high intervention price, and acquiring and stocking large amounts of rice. However, global prices started to decline as India and Viet Nam removed their export restrictions and filled the supply gap in the international market. As a result, the Thai government was left with a huge deficit and an enormous public stock of rice. The Paddy Pledging Programme was abolished in March 2014, and the government has since been trying to offload its reserves of rice. This process has become more difficult over time as the quality of rice deteriorates the longer it is kept in stock.

In November 2014, the government started the "Farmer loans to delay sales of rice paddy" programme. The objective of this programme was to stabilise the prices of fragrant and glutinous paddy by providing loans to farmers to incentivise them to delay their sales of rice paddy (GAIN-TH4120, 2014). While the original target was set at 2 million tonnes, only 350 000 tonnes were pledged in 2014/15 and 540 000 tonnes in 2015/16 (GAIN-TH6029, 2016).

Figure 1.22 illustrates for the first three periods how much rice was pledged each marketing year as well as the average intervention price for white rice. A distinction is made between main crop and off-season rice. The main crop rice interventions run from November to February, while off-season rice is acquired from March through July.[10] The fourth period is not represented in this figure as the government only acquired glutinous and fragrant rice as of 2014/15.

Figure 1.22. Rice pledging in Thailand

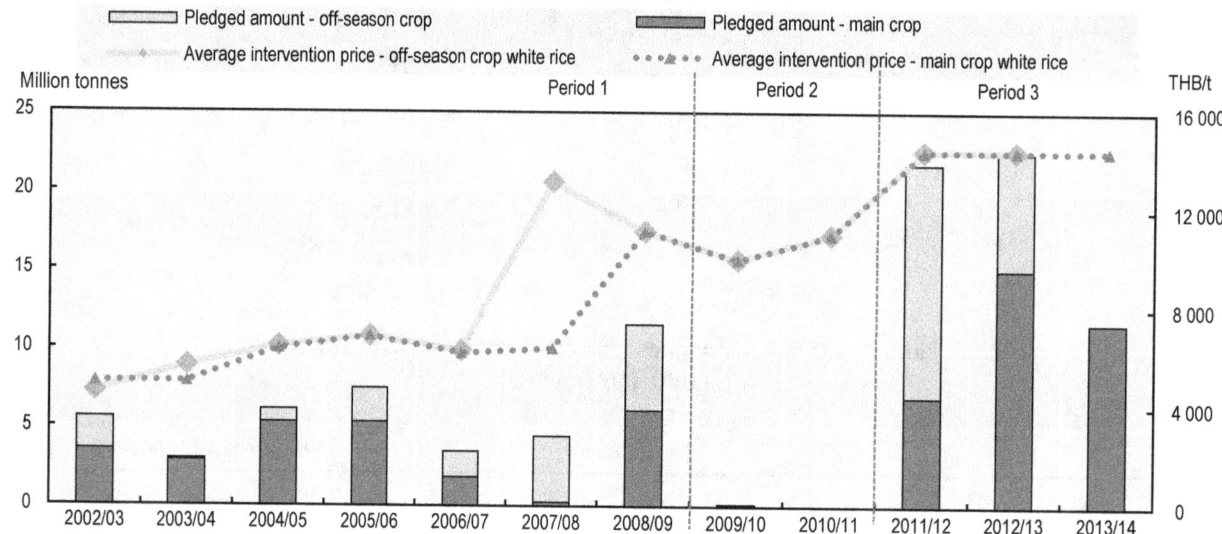

Note: During period 2, the government only acquired small amounts of rice under the Direct Purchase Programme. The intervention prices during this period correspond to the insurance prices that were set in the Price Insurance Scheme. Main crop rice is acquired between November and February, while off-season rice is acquired between March and July.
Source: Adapted from GAIN-TH4021 (2014) using data from several GAIN reports for Thailand.

Notes

[1] It is not uncommon for stockholding schemes to have multiple purposes. When these purposes are contradictory in nature, they reduce the effectiveness of the programme (World Bank, 2012).

[2] This export ban was mostly symbolic since Bangladesh exports very little rice.

[3] An exception was made for a shipment of non-fragrant rice to Sri Lanka. http://in.reuters.com/article/bangladesh-rice-srilanka-idINL4N0SM3FO20141027.

4. Boro rice is planted in December/January and harvested in April/May; Aus rice is planted in March/April and harvested in June/July; and Aman rice is planted in July/August and harvested in November/December (GAIN-BG3004, 2013).

5. All conversions to USD in this report are based on the January 2017 average monthly exchange rate.

6. AAY stands for Antyodaya Anna Yojana and refers to the poorest of the poor households in India.

7. The calculated average price is the average retail price of rice of medium standard quality during the three months before the price increase.

8. A detailed discussion of the beneficiaries of the Raskin programme can be found in OECD (2015).

9. The NFA website provides a detailed overview of the different prices: http://nfa.gov.ph/buying-selling-price.

10. In marketing year 2002/03, for example, the main crop rice was acquired between November 2002 and February 2003, while off-season rice was acquired between March 2003 and July 2003.

References

Alam, M.J., S. Akter and I.A. Begum (2015), "Effectiveness of Rice Procurement Program and the Determinants of the Farm Level Stocks of Rice in Bangladesh", International Conference of Agricultural Economists, Milan, 8-14 August.

Alam, M.J., S. Akter and I.A. Begum (2014), "Bangladesh's Rice Procurement System and Possible Alternatives in Supporting Farmer's Income and Sustaining Production Incentives", Department of Agribusiness and Marketing, Bangladesh Agricultural University, Mymensingh, May 2014.

Alavi, H.R., A. Htenas (2014), "Using Trade to Enhance Food Security in Southeast Asia", in Trade Policy and Food Security, World Bank, Washington DC, http://dx.doi.org/10.1596/978-1-4648-0305-5.

AMIS (2016), AMIS Policy Database, http://statistics.amis-outlook.org/policy/ (accessed 7 September 2016).

Banerjee, O., T. Darbas, P.R. Brown and C.H. Roth (2014), "Historical divergence in public management of food grain systems in India and Bangladesh: Opportunities to enhance food security", *Global Food Security*, Vol. 3, p. 159–166.

BERNAS (2016), Homepage of BERNAS, http://www.Bernas.com.my/ (accessed 15 September 2016).

BULOG (2016), "Sekilas Perum BULOG" [About BULOG], http://www.bulog.co.id/sekilas.php (accessed 13 September 2016).

Carter, C.A., F. Zhong and J. Zhu (2012), "Advances in Chinese Agriculture and its Global Implications", *Applied Economic Perspectives and Policy*, Vol. 34(1), 1-36. http://dx.doi.org/10.1093/aepp/ppr047.

Cheng, G. (2011), *China's Agricultural Subsidies*, China Development Press, Beijing.

Choi, S., J. Dyck and N. Childs (2016), "The Rice Market in South Korea", *Rice Outlook* No. RCS-161-01, USDA.

Commission on Audit (Republic of the Philippines) (2015), Annual Audit Report on the National Food Authority for the Year Ended 31 December 2014, Online available at: http://www.nfa.gov.ph/files/Transparency/T_COA_AAR_2014.pdf.

CountrySTAT Philippines (2017a), Palay and Corn: Volume of Production [Online consultation 28 July 2017] Available at: http://countrystat.psa.gov.ph/?cont=10&pageid=1&ma=A00PNVCP.

CountrySTAT Philippines (2017b), Agricultural Commodities: Farmgate Prices by Commodity and Year [Online consultation 28 July 2017] Available at: http://countrystat.psa.gov.ph/selection.asp.

CountrySTAT Philippines (2017c), Agricultural Commodities: Retail Prices by Commodity and Year [Online consultation 28 July 2017] Available at: http://countrystat.psa.gov.ph/selection.asp.

Department of Food and Public Distribution (FDPD), Ministry of Consumer Affairs, Food and Public Distribution, Government of India (2016), "National Food Security Act (NFSA), 2013", available at: http://dfpd.nic.in/nfsa-act.htm.

Deuss, A. (2015), "Review of the performance and impacts of recent stockholding policies", in *Issues in Agricultural Trade Policy: Proceedings of the 2014 OECD Global Forum on Agriculture*, OECD Publishing, Paris, https://doi.org/10.1787/9789264233911-5-en.

Directorate General of Food (2016), Homepage of the DGF, http://www.dgfood.gov.bd/ (accessed 26 July 2016).

Dorosh, P.A. and A. Childs (2014), "International Rice Trade and Security Stocks: Prospects for an Expanded Asian International Rice Reserve", *IFPRI Discussion Paper* 01394, International Food Policy Research Institute, Washington, D.C.

Dorosh, P. (2014), "Bangladesh Rice Stock Policy and the International Market", Presentation at Worskhop on Evidence-Based Policy Options for Food and Nutrition Security in Bangladesh, 1 October 2014, Dhaka.

DTB Associates (2014), "Agricultural subsidies in key developing countries: November 2014 update", Technical report, Available online at: http://www.farmpolicyfacts.org/wp-content/uploads/2015/02/AgriculturalSubsidies-in-Key-Developing-Countries-November-2014-Update.pdf.

FAO (2016) FAO Rice Market Monitor, several editions, Available online at:
http://www.fao.org/economic/est/publications/rice-publications/rice-market-monitor-rmm/en/.

Fernandez, L. and R. Velarde (2012), "Who Benefits from Social Assistance in the Philippines? Evidence from the Latest National Household Surveys", Philippine Social Protection Note, No. 4, World Bank Group and Australian Government Aid Program, March 2012, Online available at: http://www-wds.worldbank.org/external/default/WDSContentServer/WDSP/IB/2012/06/08/000333038_20120608041740/Rendered/PDF/694160BRI0P1180PUBLIC00FINAL0PSPN04.pdf.

Food Corporation of India (2018), Allotment and Offtake under All Schemes, Online available at:
http://fci.gov.in/sales.php?view=36.

Food Corporation of India (2016), Homepage of the Food Corporation of India, http://fci.gov.in/ (accessed 16 September 2016).

Food Planning Monitoring Unit (FPMU), Ministry of Food, People's Republic of Bangladesh (2016) (Online consultation July 2016), Available at: http://fsnis.fpmu.gov.bd/dms/advanced.html#graphcontainer.

GAIN-JA6004 (2016), "Japan: Grain and Feed Annual", USDA FAS, 15 March
http://gain.fas.usda.gov/Recent%20GAIN%20Publications/Grain%20and%20Feed%20Annual_Tokyo_Japan_3-15-2016.pdf.

GAIN-JA5009 (2015), "Japan: Grain and Feed Annual", USDA FAS, 13 March
http://gain.fas.usda.gov/Recent%20GAIN%20Publications/Grain%20and%20Feed%20Annual_Tokyo_Japan_3-13-2015.pdf.

GAIN-BG6005 (2016), "Bangladesh: Grain and Feed Annual", USDA FAS, 31 March.

GAIN-BG5003 (2015), "Bangladesh: Grain and Feed Annual", USDA FAS, 5 May.

GAIN-BG4002 (2014), "Bangladesh: Grain and Feed Annual", USDA FAS, 31 March.

GAIN-BG3004 (2013), "Bangladesh: Grain and Feed Annual", USDA FAS, 28 March.

GAIN-BG2001 (2012), "Bangladesh: Grain and Feed Annual", USDA FAS, 22 February.

GAIN-BG1101 (2011), "Bangladesh: Grain and Feed Annual", USDA FAS, 4 March.

GAIN-CH16027 (2016), "China – Peoples Republic of: Grain and Feed Annual", USDA FAS, 8 April.

GAIN-CH15014 (2015), "China – Peoples Republic of: Grain and Feed Annual", USDA FAS, 8 May.

GAIN-CH13015 (2013), "China – Peoples Republic of: Grain and Feed Annual", USDA FAS, 29 March.

GAIN-CH8012 (2008), "China – Peoples Republic of: Grain and Feed Annual", USDA FAS, 1 March.

GAIN-ID1610 (2016), "Indonesia: Grain and Feed Annual", USDA FAS, 30 March.

GAIN-ID1412 (2014), "Indonesia: GOI New regulation on rice exports and imports", USDA FAS, 6 May.

GAIN-ID1318 (2013), "Indonesia: Grain and Feed Annual", USDA FAS, 11 April.

GAIN-KS1613 (2016), "Korea – Republic of: Grain and Feed Annual", USDA FAS, 30 March.

GAIN-KS1511 (2015), "Korea – Republic of: Grain and Feed Annual", USDA FAS, 1 April.

GAIN-KS1417 (2014), "Korea – Republic of: Grain and Feed Annual", USDA FAS, 2 April.

GAIN-KS1323 (2013), "Korea – Republic of: Grain and Feed Annual", USDA FAS, 2 April.

GAIN-KS1230 (2012), "Korea – Republic of: Grain and Feed Annual", USDA FAS, 17 April.

GAIN-KS1121 (2011), "Korea – Republic of: Grain and Feed Annual", USDA FAS, 6 May.

GAIN-KS1014 (2010), "Korea – Republic of: Grain and Feed Annual", USDA FAS, 3 May.

GAIN-TH6029 (2016), "Thailand – Grain and Feed Annual", USDA FAS, 18 March.

GAIN-TH5030 (2015), "Thailand – Grain and Feed Annual", USDA FAS, 19 March.

GAIN-TH4120 (2014), "Thailand – Grain and Feed Update", USDA FAS, 4 December.

GAIN-TH4021 (2014), "Thailand – Grain and Feed Annual", USDA FAS, 7 March.

GAIN-TH1035 (2011), "Thailand – Grain and Feed Annual", USDA FAS, 22 March.

GAIN-TH9161 (2009), "Thailand – Price Insurance Starts to Replace Mortgage Scheme", USDA FAS, 29 October.

Gale, F. (2013), "U.S. Exports Surge as China Supports Agricultural Prices", USDA, 24 October 2013, http://www.ers.usda.gov/amber-waves/2013-october/us-exports-surge-as-china-supports-agricultural-prices.aspx#.V5hru01f3cs.

Government of India (2016), "Entire Country gets National Food Security Act coverage", Press Information Bureau, Ministry of Consumer Affairs, Food & Public Distribution, as on 03.11.2016, http://pib.nic.in/newsite/PrintRelease.aspx?relid=153217.

Grain Management Act (2015), Act No.11230, 26 January 2012, enforced 1 January 2015.

NFA (2013) Annual Accomplishment Report 2013, Online available at: http://www.nfa.gov.ph/files/Transparency/AAR2013.pdf.

MAFF (2016a) Demand and Supply of Government-Owed Rice, Wheat and Barley (in Japanese), Tokyo, http://www.maff.go.jp/e/tokei/kikaku/nenji_e/89nenji/index.html.

MAFF (2016b), Current situation of rice (in Japanese), Tokyo, Online available at: http://www.maff.go.jp/j/seisan/kikaku/pdf/ref_data3.pdf.

MAFF (2016c), Monthly report of rice (in Japanese), Tokyo, Online available at: http://www.maff.go.jp/j/seisan/keikaku/soukatu/pdf/mr160705.pdf.

MAFRA (2015), Notification 2015-133 (in Korean).

MAFRA (2014), Notification 2014-261 (in Korean).

Maybank IB Research (2011), "Rice + dividends = staple + stable", Online available at: http://maybank.xinhua08.com/yjbg/201108/P020110825403526661156.pdf.

NFA (2016a), Homepage of the National Food Authority, http://www.nfa.gov.ph (accessed 15 June 2016).

NFA (2016b) NFA Palay procurement 2006-2014, Online available at: http://nfa.gov.ph/files/statistics/palayprocurement06-14.pdf.

NFA (2016c) Summary of NFA rice import arrivals 2000-2012, Online available at: http://nfa.gov.ph/files/statistics/summary.pdf.

NFA (2016d) NFA Total rice distribution 2006-2014, Online available at: http://nfa.gov.ph/files/statistics/ricedistribution06-14.pdf.

NFA (2016e) Annual Accomplishment Report 2016, Online available at: http://www.nfa.gov.ph/images/files/Transparency/2016AAR030717.pdf.

NFA (2015) Annual Accomplishment Report 2015, Online available at: http://www.nfa.gov.ph/files/Transparency/AAR2015.pdf.

NFA (2014) Annual Accomplishment Report 2014, Online available at: http://www.nfa.gov.ph/files/Transparency/AAR2014.pdf.

OECD (2017), *Agricultural Policies in the Philippines*, OECD Food and Agricultural Reviews, OECD Publishing, Paris, https://doi.org/10.1787/9789264269088-en.

OECD (2016), *Agricultural Policy Monitoring and Evaluation 2016*, OECD Publishing, Paris. http://dx.doi.org/10.1787/agr_pol-2016-en.

OECD (2009), *Evaluation of Agricultural Policy Reforms in Japan*, OECD Publishing, Paris. https://doi.org/10.1787/9789264061545-en.

OECD (2008) "Agricultural Policy Design and Implementation: A Synthesis", *OECD Food, Agriculture and Fisheries Papers*, No. 7, OECD Publishing, Paris. http://dx.doi.org/10.1787/243786286663.

OECD/FAO (2017), *OECD-FAO Agricultural Outlook 2017-2026*, OECD Publishing, Paris, https://doi.org/10.1787/agr_outlook-2017-en.

Official Gazette (2010a), "Resolution No.63/NQ-CP of December 23, 2009, on National Food Security", *Issues* No. 01-02/January 2010, available at: http://faolex.fao.org/docs/pdf/vie95278.pdf.

Official Gazette (2010b), "Decree No. 109/2010/ND-CP of November 4, 2010, on Rice Export Business", *Issues* No. 05/November 2010, available at: http://faolex.fao.org/docs/pdf/vie100805.pdf.

Poapongsakorn, N. and J. Charupong (2010), "Rent-Seeking Activities and the Political Economy of the Paddy Pledging Market Intervention Measures". A Research Study Proposed to Office of the National Anti-Corruption Commission. Thailand Development Research Institute, Bangkok.

Republic of Indonesia (2014), "Peraturan Menteri Perdagangan Republik Indonesia Nomor 19/M-DAG/PER/3/2014" [Indonesian Trade Minister Regulation number 19/M-DAG/PER/3/2014], available at http://bkp.pertanian.go.id/tinymcpuk/gambar/file/Permendag%20No%2019%20Tahun%202014_Ketentuan%20Impor%20dan%20Ekspor%20Beras%20(1).pdf.

Reserve Bank of India (2017), *Handbook of Statistics on Indian Economy 2016-17*. Available at: https://www.rbi.org.in/Scripts/PublicationsView.aspx?id=17803.

SEPO (2010), "Subsidising the National Food Authority: Is it a Good Policy?", *Policy Brief*, Senate Economic Planning Office, Philippines, www.senate.gov.ph/publications/PB%202010-12%20-%20Subsidizing%20the%20NFA.pdf.

Statistic Indonesia (2016), "Average of Unhusked Rice Price by Quality, Component and GPP at Farmer in Indonesia, 2008 – 2016", https://www.bps.go.id/linkTabelStatis/view/id/1589 (accessed 13 December 2016).

Tobias, A., I. Molina, H.G. Valera, K.A. Mottaleb and S. Mohanty (2012), *Handbook on Rice Policy for Asia*, International Rice Research Institute, Los Baños (Philippines).

USDA (2015), "Trans-Pacific Partnership: Benefits to U.S. Agriculture", 20 October, Online available at: http://www.fas.usda.gov/sites/default/files/2015-10/tpp_details_rice_10-20-15.pdf.

van Tongeren, F. (2008), "Agricultural Policy Design and Implementation: A Synthesis", *OECD Food, Agriculture and Fisheries Papers*, No. 7, OECD Publishing, Paris, https://doi.org/10.1787/243786286663.

World Bank (2012), "Using Public Food grain Stocks to Enhance Food Security", Report Number 71280-GLB, September.

WTO (2016), "Tariff Analysis Online", WTO Tariff Download Facility (database), http://tariffdata.wto.org/default.aspx (accessed 13 September 2016).

WTO (2014), Working Party on State Trading Enterprises, No. 14-5715, 17 October 2014.

Annex 1.A. Marketing year by country

Annex Table 1.A.1. Start date of the rice marketing year, by country

Country	Marketing year	Start date
Bangladesh	2014/2015	May 2014
China	2014/2015	July 2014
India	2014/2015	October 2014
Indonesia	2014/2015	January 2015
Japan	2014/2015	November 2014
Korea	2014/2015	November 2014
Philippines	2014/2015	July 2014
Thailand	2014/2015	January 2015

Source: Based on GAIN reports.

Chapter 2. Modelling public stockholding programmes for rice

This chapter explains how the functioning of public stockholding programmes was modelled using the OECD-FAO Aglink-Cosimo model. It describes the data, the data sources, and the assumptions made to construct the baseline projections. This baseline scenario reflects a business-as-usual scenario that assumes current stockholding policies (as described in Chapter 1) are maintained in the selected Asian countries for the entire projection period (2018 to 2030).

2.1. Modelling public stocks in Aglink-Cosimo

The main objective of this report is to examine the potential impacts of stockholding policies on domestic and international markets over the medium term. The analysis is conducted using the OECD-FAO Aglink-Cosimo model. This model is a comprehensive partial equilibrium model for global agriculture, which can simulate developments of annual market balances and prices for the main agricultural commodities.

The standard Aglink-Cosimo model does not include important policy variables related to public stockholding policies such as public stock norms or guaranteed procurement prices, nor does it distinguish between private and public stockholding. Furthermore, the stock equations are standardized for most countries.[1]

Using the information collected in Chapter 1, which describes in detail the specific functioning of public stockholding programmes for rice in eight Asian countries up to the end of 2016, the equations for these countries in Aglink-Cosimo have been adjusted to achieve the following objectives:

- Incorporate the three possible procurement and distribution channels of public stocks.
- Separate private from public stocks.
- Include stock norms, procurement prices, and subsidised prices.

Annex 2.A gives an overview of Aglink-Cosimo, describes how stocks have been modelled in other dynamic models, and explains in detail the adjusted and new equations in Aglink-Cosimo. Since the descriptions in Chapter 1 reflect the functioning of public stockholding programmes up to and including 2016, any changes thereafter are not reflected in the model.

2.2. Assumptions for baseline projections

New variables were introduced in Aglink-Cosimo in order to model the functioning of public stockholding programmes and data needed to be collected for each of them. For certain variables, time series data were available for relatively long periods of time, while there were gaps in the historic series for other variables. This section describes the assumptions made to fill these gaps, as well as the assumptions made to extend the series over the Aglink-Cosimo baseline projection period (2018-2030).

Table 2.1 lists the new variables and indicates by country which information needed to be collected. It also lists other variables that are crucial for the modelling but are already available in Aglink-Cosimo (indicated by *). For these latter variables – namely total stock volumes, producer prices, consumer prices, export prices, import prices, and trade policies – historic time series as well as data for the projection period are available in the Aglink-Cosimo database.[2]

For the new variables related to the acquisition and release of rice from public stocks, the data requirements varied by country. For example, for a country that exclusively buys domestically-produced rice at prevailing market prices, it was not necessary to collect information on procurement prices. In addition, for each country data needed to be collected on the volumes of public and private stocks, and public stock norms.

Table 2.1. Data requirements for modelling

	Bangladesh	China	India	Indonesia	Japan	Korea	Philippines	Thailand
Stock volumes								
Total stock levels*	X	X	X	X	X	X	X	X
Public stock levels	X		X	X	X	X	X	X
Public stock norms	X	X	X	X	X	X	X	X
Private stock levels	X		X	X	X	X	X	X
Trade policies								
Import policies*	X	X	X	X	X	X	X	X
Export policies*	X	X	X	X	X	X	X	X
Acquisition prices								
Producer price*					X	X		
Procurement price	X	X	X	X			X	X
Import price*	X	X		X			X	
Acquisition volumes								
At producer price					X	X		
At procurement price	X	X	X	X			X	X
At import price	X	X		X			X	
Distribution prices								
Consumer price*		X	X	X	X	X		X
Subsidized price	X		X	X			X	
Export price*			X					X
Distribution volumes								
At consumer price		X	X	X	X	X		X
At subsidized price	X		X	X			X	
At export price			X					X

Note: * Indicates variables for which data are already available in the Aglink-Cosimo database.

The projection period covers 2018-2030 and the base year was set at 2017. Several rules were implemented when collecting data for the new variables and constructing the baseline projections:

- The same source was used for historic data, i.e. the data were not combined from different sources. When multiple sources were available, the source with the most complete recent time series was selected.
- Data were converted to milled equivalent.
- For the projections of several variables a five-year average was used to capture the most recent developments in the country. For example, public stocks can be expressed as a share of total stocks and Aglink-Cosimo includes projections for total stocks. To extend public stock levels over the projection period, the average share of public stocks in total stocks over the last five years was calculated. This average share was then used to calculate public stock levels over the projection period. The five-year period ideally comprised the years 2013-2017. However, depending on data availability, an earlier or shorter period was used. The five-

year average methodology was applied when recent data did not reveal any clear trend.

- As is common practice when constructing baseline projections, it is assumed there are no policy changes over the projection period. This means that for the baseline projections, it is assumed that public stockholding programmes will function as described in Chapter 1.[3]

Chapter 3 examines how markets are affected by changes in these programmes. Other specific assumptions are described in detail below.

Stock volumes

There are four variables related to stock included in the model: total stock volume, public stock volume, private stock volume, and public stock norm. The Aglink-Cosimo database contains historic and projection data for total stock volumes. Historic public stock data were collected from the AMIS Market Database,[4] official governmental sources, and USDA'S Global Agriculture Information Network (GAIN) reports. To extend public stock data over the projection period, the share of public stocks in total stocks over the last five years was calculated and the average of this share was then maintained over the projection period. Private stock data were calculated as the difference between total stocks and public stocks. Information on the public stock norm was converted into days of national food consumption. The most recent norm figure was used for the projections. Since projections of national food consumption are included in Aglink-Cosimo, the projections of the norm follow the same trend.

Figure 2.1. Total and public stocks of rice, averages for 2018-2030

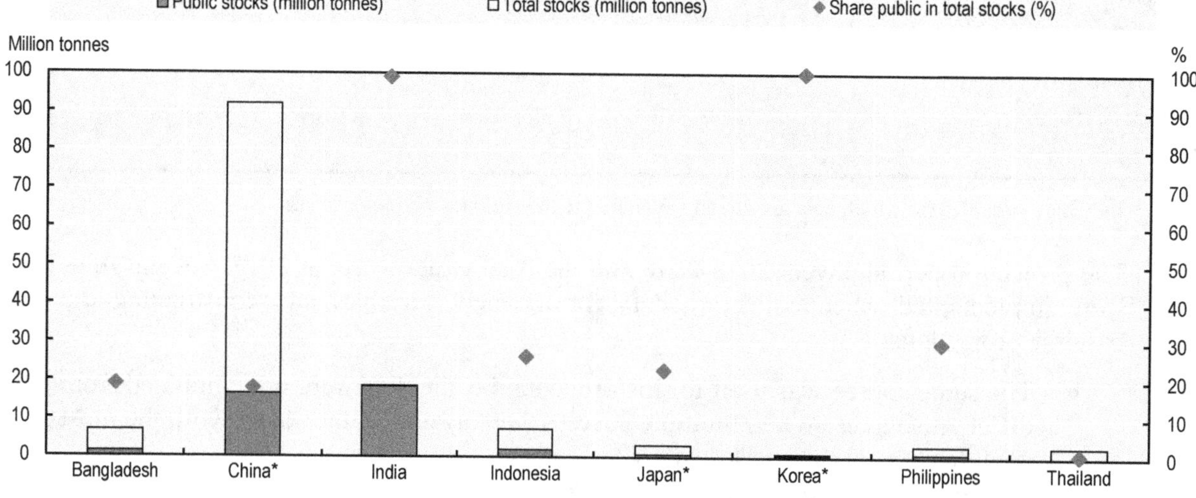

Note: * The level of public stocks in China is not based on an actual number; instead it is artificially set to the equivalent of 52 days of domestic food consumption. The choice for this level of public stocks in China is explained in the next section. Public stock data for Japan and Korea refer to public stocks composed of domestic rice. To extend public stock data over the projection period, the share of public stocks in total stocks over the last five years was calculated and the average of this share was then used over the projection period.
Source: Historic data and projections on total stock volumes are obtained from the Aglink-Cosimo database. Historic data on public stock volumes come from different sources: USDA GAIN reports for Bangladesh and Korea; AMIS Market Database for Indonesia, India, and Thailand; the Ministry of Agriculture, Forestry and Fisheries (MAFF) for Japan; and the National Food Authority (NFA) for the Philippines.

Figure 2.1 illustrates the average levels of public and total stocks as well as the average share of public stocks in total stocks over the projection period. Since the official information on the level of public stocks in China is kept confidential, the numbers are not based on historic data. For the modelling purpose, it was assumed that China's public stock level is equivalent to 52 days of national consumption. This number was artificially selected for reasons explained in the next section.

There are no private stocks in Korea (GAIN-KS1804, 2018), which implies that total stocks equal government stocks. In India, almost all rice stocks are held by the government. The private sector has been marginalised from stockholding activities as a result of the government's huge public stock programme which has discouraged the private sector from participating. In addition, private stockholding is limited under the Essential Commodities Act (1955).

The public stock data for Japan and Korea in Figure 2.1 refer to public stocks composed of domestic rice. As described in Chapter 1, there are two types of public stocks in these countries. The first type is composed of domestically produced rice, while the second one is built with imported rice. The amount of rice in the second type of public stocks depends on the countries' respective Tariff Rate Quota (TRQ) levels. In recent years, the TRQs for both countries have been filled and it is assumed this will continue over the projection period. Since the amount of rice in the second type of public stock is assumed to remain constant, this stock is excluded from the modelling of public stock scenarios. Furthermore, in Japan public stocks of imported rice are rarely used for domestic food consumption and the amounts are relatively small. Any change in public stock levels under the scenario analysis in these two countries hence occurs strictly via the first type of public stocks (composed of domestically-produced rice). Consequently, all graphs and modelling results related to public stocks in Chapters 2 and 3 refer to the first type of stock. The second type of stocks is incorporated in the total stock volumes for both countries.

Public stock levels in Thailand are projected to be almost zero during the projection period. This reflects the government's stockholding policy in 2016, whereby it planned to liquidate remaining public stocks during 2017 and started to encourage the private sector to hold stocks (FAO, 2017a; GAIN-THA8020, 2018; GAIN-THA7011, 2018).

Procurement volumes

Rice for public stocks can be procured domestically or internationally. Historic data on domestic procurement is obtained from official government sources, OECD, and USDA GAIN reports. For most countries, projections for domestic procurement volumes are obtained by calculating the average share of procurement in total production during the five most recent years. This share is then applied to the rice production data (already in Aglink-Cosimo) to obtain procurement volumes for the projection period. Table 2.2 lists these shares and the sources for historic data on procurement.

In Japan, projections for domestic procurement were obtained differently. Specifically, domestic procurement is set by the government at 200 000 tonnes of brown rice per year. This is equivalent to 181 200 tonnes of milled rice, using the conversion factor of 0.906 (MAFF, 2015). There is no information on procurement volumes for either Thailand (no public stocks during baseline projection) or China.

Rice for public stocks can also be imported. For those countries that regularly use imported rice to build public stocks, the baseline projections were obtained by calculating the average share of imports in total procurement for the last five years and then applying this share over the projection period. The other countries in the study have occasionally imported rice to add to their public stocks. In the model, these imports are modelled to occur when the domestic to international price ratio exceeds a certain threshold.

Table 2.2. Sources for procurement data and average share of domestic procurement in total production (2018-2030)

Country	Source for historic data on procurement	Average share of domestic procurement in total production (2018-2030)
Bangladesh	Food Planning Monitoring Unit (FPMU, 2017)	4%
China	n.a.	n.a.
India	Reserve Bank of India (RBI, 2017)	32%
Indonesia	OECD (2015) and GAIN reports	6%
Japan	Ministry of Agriculture, Forestry and Fisheries (MAFF)	2%
Korea	GAIN reports	13%
Philippines	National Food Authority (NFA, 2016a, 2016b, 2017)	1%
Thailand	n.a.	n.a.

Distribution volumes

Rice from public stocks can be released on the international market (exports) or on the domestic market at either market prices or subsidised prices. The total amount of rice distributed from public stocks each year was calculated residually. The formula used is:

$$distributed_t = [(1 - loss) * publicstock_{t-1}] + procured_t - publicstock_t$$

The baseline projections used the historic information on the share of public stocks released through the three different channels. For example, if during the last five years a country released on average 10% of public stocks on the domestic market at the prevailing market prices and 90% on the domestic market at subsidised prices, then these same percentages were applied for the projections. Figure 2.2 shows these shares for the projection period. China and Thailand are not included in these graphs because China has no data on procurement and distribution volumes, and Thailand does not build public stocks of rice under the baseline scenario. India has historically exported rice from its public stocks, but these shares have been minimal in the most recent years. This explains why the share of exports is practically zero for India over the projection period.

**Figure 2.2. Average relative shares of public stocks
released on the domestic and international markets, 2018-2030**

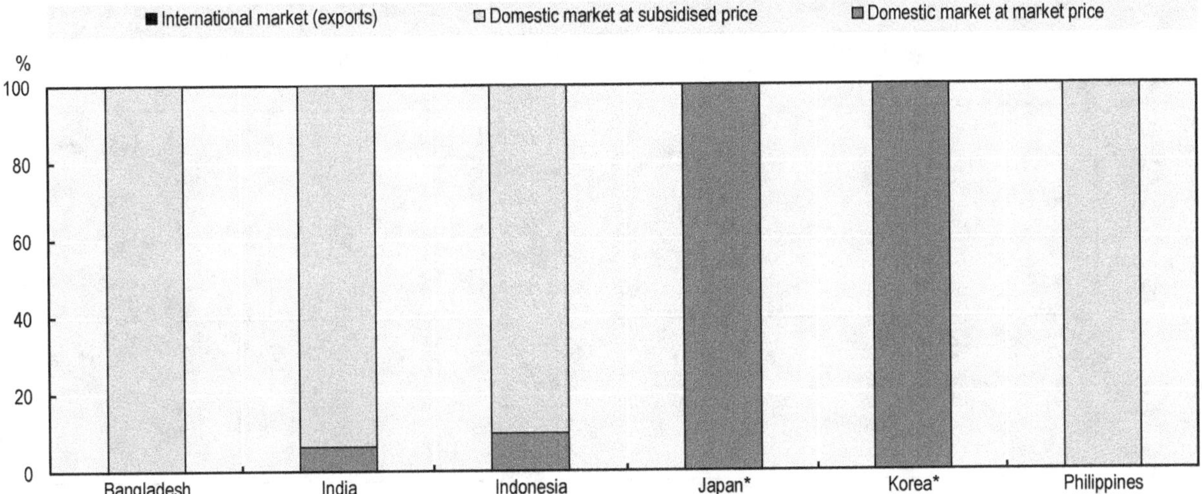

* Public stock data in Japan and Korea refer to public stocks composed of domestic rice. Relative shares of the different distribution channels during the projection period are based on historic shares. Release on the international market is minimal under the baseline for the countries in the figure.
Source: Historic relative shares from Food Corporation of India (2018) for India and GAIN Reports for Indonesia.

Prices

Six sets of prices are crucial for the modelling. Four are already included in Aglink-Cosimo, namely: producer, consumer, import, and export prices.[5] The producer prices in Aglink-Cosimo are derived from wholesale prices, while the consumer prices are derived from retail prices. The producer and consumer prices in Aglink-Cosimo were cross-checked with wholesale and retail price series in GIEWS (2018) and, where necessary, adjustments were made to the Aglink-Cosimo data.

Historic information on procurement prices and subsidised consumer prices was collected from several sources. When multiple price series were available, one series was selected or an average was calculated. Table 2.3 explains how the procurement and subsidised prices were obtained and lists the sources.

For the baseline projections, the procurement price in each country is assumed to follow a trend reflecting its recent relationship with the domestic producer price. The procurement price is assumed to remain below the producer price. Subsidised consumer prices are assumed to remain constant in nominal terms, which is consistent with the overall trend in those countries. Figure 2.3 illustrates the relationship between the producer, consumer, procurement, and subsidised prices for each country in the study.

Figure 2.3. Consumer, producer, procurement and subsidised prices of rice, 2000-2030

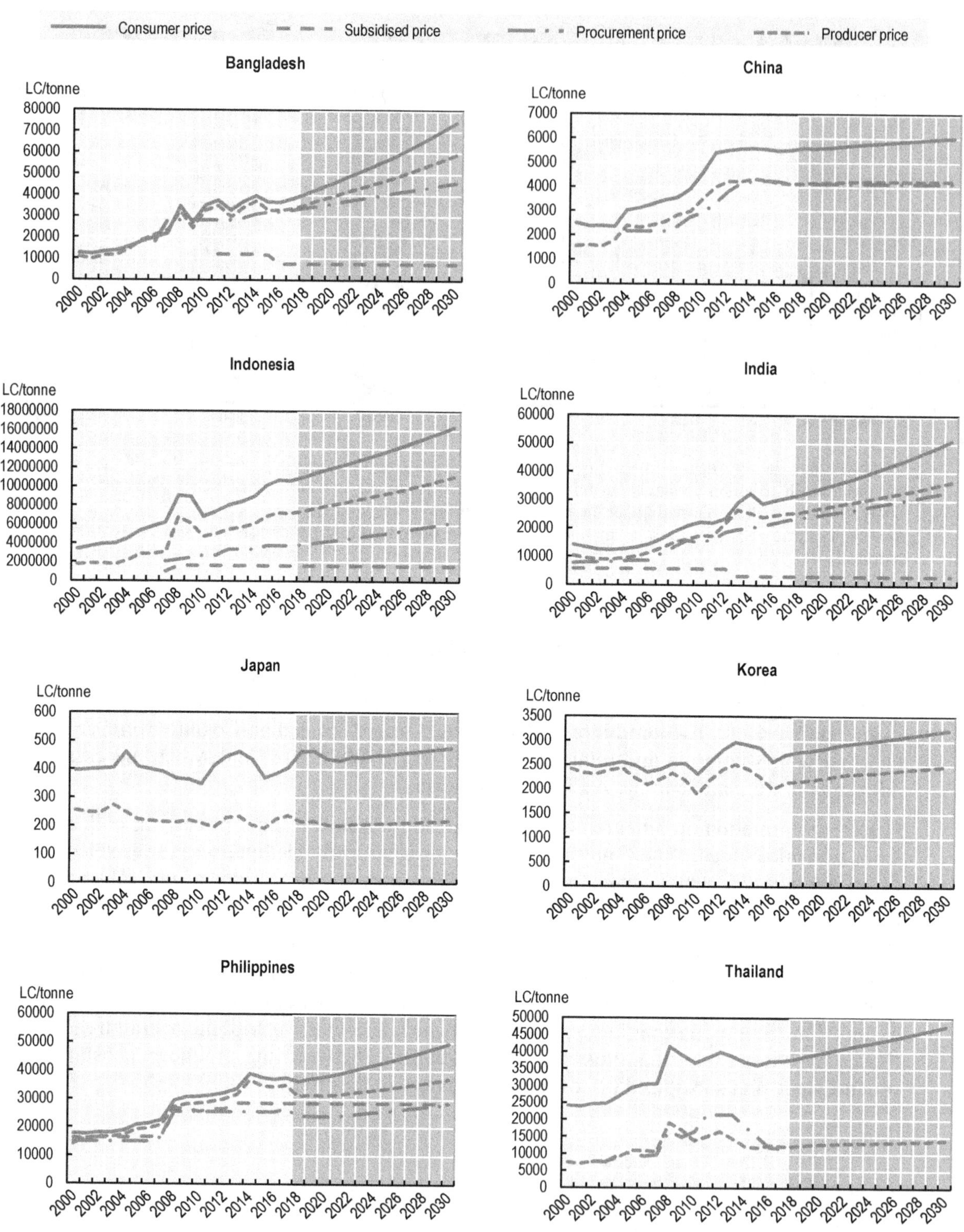

Note: All prices are in milled equivalent. Shaded area indicates the projection period 2018-2030.
Source: Aglink-Cosimo for producer and consumer prices. Table 2.3 lists the sources for procurement and subsidised prices.

Table 2.3. Selected procurement and subsidised consumer prices

	Procurement price		Subsidised consumer price	
	Selected series	Source	Selected series	Source
Bangladesh	Weighted average of procurement prices during Boro and Aman harvests, weighted by actual procurement levels	Food Planning Monitoring Unit (FPMU, 2017)	Simple average of free and subsidised price	FAO (2017b)
China	Simple average of paddy procurement prices for early indica, late/intermediate indica and japonica	GAIN reports for China	n.a.	
Indonesia	Wet paddy at milling level	GAIN reports for Indonesia	Subsidised price	GAIN reports for Indonesia
India	Minimum support price of paddy	Reserve Bank of India (2017)	Subsidised price	Reserve Bank of India (2017)
Philippines	NFA support price	NFA (2018)	Simple average of the four NFA selling prices of rice	NFA (2018)
Thailand	Main crop white rice	GAIN reports for Thailand	n.a.	

Note: Paddy prices were converted to milled equivalent.

2.3. Limitations of the model and data

When examining the baseline and other scenarios, it is important to keep in mind the limitations of the model and data. First, the modelling of stockholding programmes is based on the description given in Chapter 1, and thus this report does not take into account how stockholding policies changed in 2017 or thereafter. Second, there are many varieties of rice which differ considerably. Aglink-Cosimo does not separate between these varieties and uses a single aggregate figure. Third, the parameters in the model are not based on estimates, but are selected based on plausibility considerations and the literature. Fourth, even though stocks and other variables can vary significantly within a year, it is not possible to do any intra-annual analysis since the data and model are annual.

Notes

[1] These equations are described in the documentation of the Aglink-Cosimo model, http://www.agri-outlook.org/abouttheoutlook/Aglink-Cosimo-model-documentation-2015.pdf

[2] Aglink-Cosimo data were obtained from the *OECD-FAO Agricultural Outlook 2017-2026* and extended to 2030.

[3] Chapter 1 describes the functioning of public stockholding programmes up to the end of 2016.

[4] http://www.amis-outlook.org/database/market-database/en/

[5] Detailed information on these prices can be found in the documentation of the Aglink-Cosimo model, http://www.agri-outlook.org/abouttheoutlook/Aglink-Cosimo-model-documentation-2015.pdf

References

AMIS (2016), AMIS Policy Database, http://statistics.amis-outlook.org/policy/ (accessed 7 February 2018).

FAO (2017a), *Rice Market Monitor July 2017*, Trade and Markets Division Food and Agriculture Organization of the United Nations, vol. 20(2), pp. 1–35, http://www.fao.org/fileadmin/templates/est/COMM_MARKETS_MONITORING/Rice/Images/RMM/RMM-Jul17.pdf.

FAO (2017b), *Commodity Policy Developments Tool*, http://www.fao.org/economic/est/est-commodities/commodity-policy-archive/en/ (last accessed December 2017).

Food Corporation of India (2018), "Homepage of the Food Corporation of India" (FCI), http://fci.gov.in/ (last accessed February 2018).

Food Planning Monitoring Unit (FPMU), Ministry of Food, People's Republic of Bangladesh (2017) (Online consultation November 2017), Available at: http://fsnis.fpmu.gov.bd/dms/advanced.html#graphcontainer.

GAIN-BG6005 (2016), "Bangladesh: Grain and Feed Annual", USDA FAS, 31 March.

GAIN-BG5003 (2015), "Bangladesh: Grain and Feed Annual", USDA FAS, 5 May.

GAIN-BG4002 (2014), "Bangladesh: Grain and Feed Annual", USDA FAS, 31 March.

GAIN-BG3004 (2013), "Bangladesh: Grain and Feed Annual", USDA FAS, 28 March.

GAIN-BG2001 (2012), "Bangladesh: Grain and Feed Annual", USDA FAS, 22 February.

GAIN-BG1101 (2011), "Bangladesh: Grain and Feed Annual", USDA FAS, 4 March.

GAIN-CH17017 (2017), "China – Peoples Republic of: Grain and Feed Annual", USDA FAS, 4 April.

GAIN-CH16027 (2016), "China – Peoples Republic of: Grain and Feed Annual", USDA FAS, 8 April.

GAIN-CH15014 (2015), "China – Peoples Republic of: Grain and Feed Annual", USDA FAS, 8 May.

GAIN-CH13015 (2013), "China – Peoples Republic of: Grain and Feed Annual", USDA FAS, 29 March.

GAIN-CH8012 (2008), "China – Peoples Republic of: Grain and Feed Annual", USDA FAS, 1 March.

GAIN-ID1707 (2017), "Indonesia: Grain and Feed Annual", USDA FAS, 30 March.

GAIN-ID1610 (2016), "Indonesia: Grain and Feed Annual", USDA FAS, 30 March.

GAIN-ID1412 (2014), "Indonesia: GOI New regulation on rice exports and imports", USDA FAS, 6 May.

GAIN-ID1318 (2013), "Indonesia: Grain and Feed Annual", USDA FAS, 11 April.

GAIN-KS1804 (2018), "Korea – Republic of: Grain and Feed Update", USDA FAS, 29 January.

GAIN-KS1613 (2016), "Korea – Republic of: Grain and Feed Annual", USDA FAS, 30 March.

GAIN-KS1511 (2015), "Korea – Republic of: Grain and Feed Annual", USDA FAS, 1 April.

GAIN-KS1417 (2014), "Korea – Republic of: Grain and Feed Annual", USDA FAS, 2 April.

GAIN-KS1323 (2013), "Korea – Republic of: Grain and Feed Annual", USDA FAS, 2 April.

GAIN-KS1230 (2012), "Korea – Republic of: Grain and Feed Annual", USDA FAS, 17 April.

GAIN-KS1121 (2011), "Korea – Republic of: Grain and Feed Annual", USDA FAS, 6 May.

GAIN-KS1014 (2010), "Korea – Republic of: Grain and Feed Annual", USDA FAS, 3 May.

GAIN-TH8020 (2018), "Thailand – Grain and Feed Update", USDA FAS, 26 January.

GAIN-TH7011 (2018), "Thailand – Rice Market and Policy changes over the Past Decade", USDA FAS, 18 January.

GAIN-TH6029 (2016), "Thailand – Grain and Feed Annual", USDA FAS, 18 March.

GAIN-TH5030 (2015), "Thailand – Grain and Feed Annual", USDA FAS, 19 March.

GAIN-TH4120 (2014), "Thailand – Grain and Feed Update", USDA FAS, 4 December.

GAIN-TH4021 (2014), "Thailand – Grain and Feed Annual", USDA FAS, 7 March.

GAIN-TH1035 (2011), "Thailand – Grain and Feed Annual", USDA FAS, 22 March.

GAIN-TH9161 (2009), "Thailand – Price Insurance Starts to Replace Mortgage Scheme", USDA FAS, 29 October.

GIEWS (2018) Food Price Monitoring and Analysis Tool, http://www.fao.org/giews/food-prices/tool/public/ (accessed February 2018).

Hertel T., J. Reimer and E. Valenzuela (2003), "Incorporating Commodity Stockholding Behavior into a Short-run General Equilibrium Model of the Global Economy", Prepared for presentation at the joint meetings of the American Agricultural Economics Association, Canadian Agricultural Economics Society, and Rural Sociological Society, 27-30 July 2003, Montreal, Quebec.

Kozicka M., M. Kalkuhl and J. Brockhaus (2017), "Food Grain Policies and their Implications for Stocks and Fiscal Costs: A Dynamic Partial Equilibrium Analysis", *Journal of Agricultural Economics*, Vol. 68(1): 98-122(25), https://doi.org/10.1111/1477-9552.12176.

MAFF (2016a), "Demand and Supply of Government-Owed Rice, Wheat and Barley" (in Japanese), Tokyo, http://www.maff.go.jp/e/tokei/kikaku/nenji_e/89nenji/index.html.

MAFF (2016b), "Current Situation of Rice" (in Japanese), Tokyo, Online available at: http://www.maff.go.jp/j/seisan/kikaku/pdf/ref_data3.pdf.

MAFF (2016c), *Monthly Report of Rice* (in Japanese), Tokyo, Online available at: http://www.maff.go.jp/j/seisan/keikaku/soukatu/pdf/mr160705.pdf.

MAFF (2015), *Monthly Report of Rice*, March 2015 (in Japanese), Tokyo, Online available at: http://www.maff.go.jp/j/seisan/keikaku/soukatu/attach/pdf/mr-20.pdf.

NFA (2018), Homepage of the National Food Authority, http://www.nfa.gov.ph (last accessed February 2018).

NFA (2017) NFA Palay Procurement 2011-2016, available at: http://nfa.gov.ph/images/files/statistics/palayprocurement.pdf.

NFA (2016a) NFA Palay Procurement 2006-2014, available at: http://nfa.gov.ph/files/statistics/palayprocurement06-14.pdf.

NFA (2016b) Summary of NFA Rice Import Arrivals 2000-2012, available at: http://nfa.gov.ph/files/statistics/summary.pdf.

NFA (2016d) NFA Total Rice Distribution 2006-2014, available at: http://nfa.gov.ph/files/statistics/ricedistribution06-14.pdf.

NFA (2015) *Annual Accomplishment Report 2015*, available at: http://www.nfa.gov.ph/files/Transparency/AAR2015.pdf.

NFA (2014) *Annual Accomplishment Report 2014*, available at: http://www.nfa.gov.ph/files/Transparency/AAR2014.pdf.

OECD/ICRIER (2018), *Agricultural Policies in India*, OECD Food and Agricultural Reviews, OECD Publishing, Paris, https://doi.org/10.1787/9789264302334-en.

OECD (2015), *Managing Food Insecurity Risk: Analytical Framework and Application to Indonesia*, OECD Publishing, Paris. http://dx.doi.org/10.1787/9789264233874-en.

OECD (2012), *OECD Review of Agricultural Policies: Indonesia 2012*, OECD Publishing.
http://dx.doi.org/10.1787/9789264179011-en.

Reserve Bank of India (2017), *Handbook of Statistics on Indian Economy 2016-17*, available at:
https://www.rbi.org.in/Scripts/PublicationsView.aspx?id=17803.

Annex 2.A. Adjustments in Aglink-Cosimo

Overview of the Aglink-Cosimo model

The analysis undertaken in this study uses the 2017 version of the Aglink-Cosimo model.[1] Aglink-Cosimo is a recursive-dynamic, partial equilibrium model used to simulate developments of annual market balances and prices for the main agricultural commodities produced, consumed, and traded worldwide. It is managed by the Secretariats of the OECD and the Food and Agriculture Organization of the United Nations (FAO), and used to generate the *OECD-FAO Agricultural Outlook* and for policy scenario analysis. Aglink-Cosimo covers the whole world and projections are developed and maintained by the OECD and FAO Secretariats in conjunction with country experts and national administrations. Several key factors and assumptions are listed below.

- World markets for agricultural commodities are competitive, with buyers and sellers acting as price takers. Market prices are determined through a global or regional equilibrium in supply and demand.

- Domestically-produced and traded commodities are assumed to be homogeneous and thus perfect substitutes by buyers and sellers. In particular, importers do not distinguish between commodities by country of origin as Aglink-Cosimo is not a spatial model. Imports and exports are nevertheless determined separately. The homogeneity assumption extends to the rice market, but some heterogeneity is accounted for by assuming a lower substitutability of domestic production and imports in countries with high shares of Japonica rice consumption.

- Aglink-Cosimo is a partial equilibrium model for the main agricultural commodities. Non-agricultural markets are not modelled (except for the biofuel sector) and are treated exogenously to the model. Therefore, hypotheses concerning the paths of key macroeconomic variables are predetermined and there is no feedback from developments in agricultural markets to the economy as a whole.

- Aglink-Cosimo is recursive-dynamic. Consequently, each year is modelled over the projection period and depends on the outcome of previous years. Aglink-Cosimo simulates generally ten years into the future with a version available until 2030. This latter version is used in the current study.

The upper part of Figure 2.A1 provides a general overview of one domestic commodity market in Aglink-Cosimo with the main linkages between endogenous and exogenous variables.

Supply and demand are balanced by clearing for a domestic price. This price is an important explanatory variable in each of the supply and demand components. The supply side consists of three major elements: production, imports, and beginning stocks (which are equal to the ending stocks of the previous year). Production equations are not only influenced by the endogenous domestic price, but also by exogenous variables, such as energy prices, weather conditions, and domestic policies. Imports of a commodity are a function of the ratio between domestic and international prices as well as trade policies.

Demand is composed of food use, feed use, other use, exports, and ending stocks. Food use equations depend on demographics, real income developments, and the consumer price ratios between the commodities of the food basket. Feed use quantities depend on the price ratios between the different feed bulk commodities, but also on the production quantities of the animal products using this feed. Depending on the commodity, the category "other use" might be broken down into sub-categories,[2] but in general includes other industrial uses and losses occurring along the supply chains. Exports are – like imports – a function of the ratio between international and domestic prices and of trade policies.

Figure 2.A1. Aglink-Cosimo model with stock equation extensions

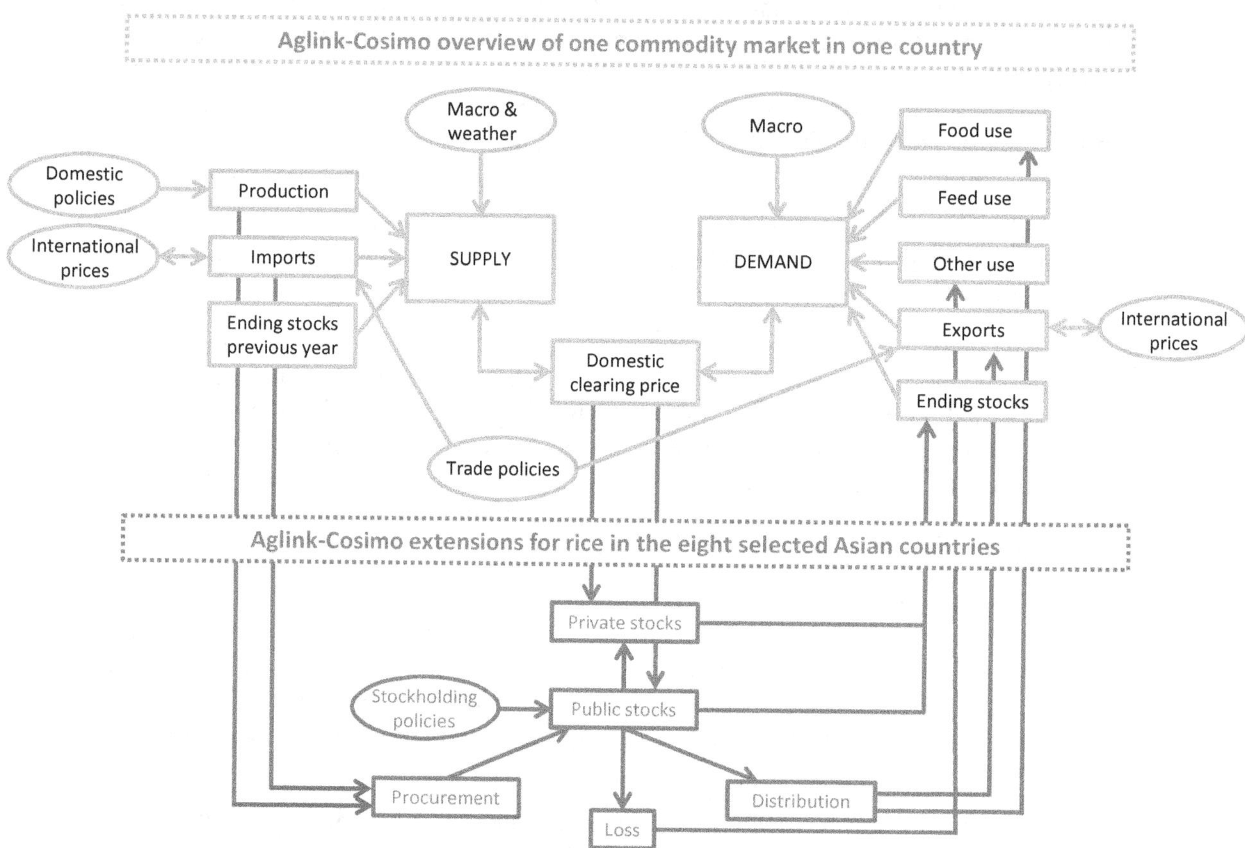

Note: The rectangular shapes contain the endogenous variables while the oval shapes indicate the exogenous variables.

Modelling of stocks in dynamic models

Only recursive dynamic models can be used to trace the behaviour of annual stock variables. Comparative static models usually simulate a stable equilibrium that is not influenced by annual fluctuations and thus are unable to address short-term variations. In addition to Aglink-Cosimo, commonly used dynamic models are the global models developed by the Food and Agriculture Policy Research Institute (FAPRI) and by the

Economic Research Service (ERS) of the United States Department of Agriculture, as well as some Computable General Equilibrium (CGE) models.

Most stock equations in Aglink-Cosimo have the same structure. Ending stocks are modelled according to the principle that stocks of a specific commodity are built when the price of this commodity falls below a certain threshold, when supply is high or demand is low. The price considered is the producer price and the threshold is the average producer price of the previous three years. Conversely, stocks are released when the price is higher than the threshold, supply is low or demand is high. Specifically, the stocks of a specific commodity in a specific country at a specific time are modelled as follows in Aglink-Cosimo (subscripts are omitted to improve the legibility):

$$LN(ST) = \alpha_{ST} + \beta_{ST,QP} * LN(QP + ST(-1)) + \beta_{ST,QC} * LN(QC)$$
$$+\beta_{ST,PP} * \frac{3*PP}{PP(-1)+PP(-2)+PP(-3)} + \beta_{ST,TRD} * TRD$$

Where:

ST: ending stocks

QP: quantity produced

QC: quantity consumed

PP: producer price (domestic clearing price)

TRD: trend

α, β: equation-specific coefficients

The above equation reflects private stockholding behaviour although the data in the model relates to total stocks, which includes both private and public stocks. For India and China, additional equations related to public rice stocks are specified. In India, stock procurement also occurs when stock levels are below a specified norm or when the producer price is below the minimum support price. In both cases, rice is assumed to be procured from domestic producers. China is modelled to import rice when its stock level falls below a specified norm.

In the FAPRI stochastic model, there is no single specification of the stock equations.[3] For most crops, stocks are a function of the commodity price and of one or multiple supply variables. These supply variables differ across commodities and countries. In some cases only production is considered, while in others beginning stocks or imports are included. Production in the next year (period $t+1$) is used as an additional explanatory variable since it is assumed that in the months before the harvest the market actors already have a good estimate of the size of the crop. As a result, prices and stocks adjust accordingly. For example, in the case of a drought, the production in period $t+1$ is expected to be lower, which will motivate market actors to hold onto stocks, which in turn will drive up prices in period t. In addition, public stockholding policies are incorporated in certain cases. One example is the US nine-month loan programme which provides a storage subsidy. Separate equations for stocks under that programme exist and imperfect substitution with commercial stocks is assumed.

The USDA outlook model used at ERS represents stocks in different ways, depending on the country and the commodity. There are cases where stocks are just an identity and other cases where demand for stockholding is treated as a function of prices and trends. In the case of big importers, stocks are a function of consumption and domestic prices. Policy variables also occur in some cases (e.g. India). In general, stocks are drawn down when weather-induced supply shortfalls result in rising prices. The incidence of weather-induced movement in stocks is more prevalent in countries with highly variable precipitation, or no or limited irrigation capacity (e.g. North Africa). When such countries are modelled, yield is considered the best predictor of stocks. Unfortunately no publicly available documentation of these equations exists.

Most dynamic CGE models focus on long run growth effects and not on short run issues like stockholding behaviour. Hertel et al. (2003) introduced a simple stock behaviour equation as a function of expected revenues and costs from stockholding as well as max and min conditions on stock levels. The authors tried to improve the validation of CGE models, considered as one of their main limitations, by generating stochastic experiments and comparing the price and stock variations to those historically observed.

Even though some of the global models listed above distinguish to a certain extent between private and public stockholding behaviour, none contain the envisaged detail of stock modelling required for the analysis in this study. These requirements are: i) separate private from public stocks; ii) incorporate the three possible procurement and distribution channels of public stocks; and iii) include stock norms, procurement prices and subsidised prices. In the current literature only one model was identified which includes some of these requirements. Kozicka et al. (2016) developed a partial equilibrium model for rice and wheat to analyse the stockholding system in India. They introduced a distinction between private and public stocks, and model private stocks as a function of commodity supply and the level of public stocks. The way in which the authors incorporated how the level of public stock affects private stocks, i.e. the crowding out effect, has been incorporated in the revised stock equations in Aglink-Cosimo (see below). Their model also distinguishes between the procurement and distributional aspects of stockholding behaviour and incorporates policy variables such as minimum support prices, subsidised prices, and stock norms.

Adjustments to rice stockholding equations in Aglink-Cosimo

As explained above, the standard Aglink-Cosimo model does not include important policy variables such as stock norms or procurement prices, does not separate public from private stocks, nor does it distinguish between the different channels of procurement and distribution of public stocks. In addition, the stock equations are standardised for most countries. This section explains how the equations in Aglink-Cosimo have been adjusted to incorporate this information for the countries in this study.

The lower part of Figure 2.A1 summarises the extensions made for rice in the eight countries of this study. The ending stock equation is replaced by two separate equations: one for private stocks and another for public stocks. Private stocks are mainly market-driven as indicated by their link with the domestic clearing price, and are also influenced by public stocks through the crowding out effect. Public stocks have additional policy variables that determine their behaviour and are influenced by procurement activities, distribution activities, and loss. Procurement can occur on the domestic market (production) or the international market (imports), and distribution can also take place in the domestic market (food use) or the international market (exports).[4] Losses from public stockholding activities are linked to the component "other use", and, more specifically, to the sub-category of this variable that covers losses along the value chains.

In the equations below, the commodity and country subscripts are omitted to improve their legibility. All these equations apply to rice and are activated for the eight countries in the study. Furthermore, all the behavioural functions include a calibration factor which is not explicitly specified in the equations below. This factor is used to calibrate the model equations to the baseline projections for all stock-related variables. As explained in Chapter 2, these baseline projections were obtained using specific rules and are based on the 2017 version of the Aglink-Cosimo model. Hence, the values for the new stock-related variables were created according to the rules specified in Chapter 2 and the model equations (specified below) were calibrated to those values using the equation-specific calibration factors. More specifically, this calibration is done by plugging the projected values into the left hand sides of the equations, then solving the equations for the equation-specific calibration factors, and finally calculating their values.

Total stocks

Total stocks (ST) are the sum of private (PRST) and public stocks (PUST).

$$ST = PRST + PUST$$

Private stocks

Private stocks follow the "buy low – sell high" principle. If the current market price (PP) is above the average of the previous three years, then stocks decrease and vice versa. In addition, it is assumed that public stocks can crowd out private stockholding to a certain extent, which means that private stocks decrease as public stocks increase. As mentioned above, this behaviour was based on Kozicka et al. (2016). However, whereas Kozicka et al. (2016) use available supply as an explanatory variable, this study uses the price ratio instead. Since supply and prices are linked – with higher supply triggering lower prices and vice versa – the price ratio is considered a better proxy for the potential benefits of buying and selling rice from private stocks.

$$LN(PRST) = \alpha_{PRST} + \beta_{PRST,PP}\, LN\left(\frac{3 * PP}{PP(-1) + PP(-2) + PP(-3)}\right) + \beta_{PRST,PUSTN}\, LN(PUSTN)$$

Price ratio elasticities ($\beta_{PRST,PP}$) average around -0.8 and crowding out elasticities ($\beta_{PRST,PUSTN}$) range between -0.05 and -0.2 for the eight countries.

The crowding out behaviour of private stocks by public stocks has been linked to the stock norm, rather than to the total public stock level. The reason for this is that in a situation with a one year shock (as with the simulated yield shock in the analysis) it is most likely that the actors holding private storage realise that the reduced public stock levels are only a temporary deviation from the equilibrium and thus they do not start to increase procurement. Therefore, only price ratios explain private stock change in this situation.[5]

Public stock levels

Public stock levels depend on four components:

1. a behavioural equation (PUST..EQ) reflecting similar price behaviour as in the private stock case, but with lower elasticities,

2. a component that activates additional procurement (PRCU..ADD) as soon as the market price falls 10% below the procurement price (MSP),[6]

3. the 90% of the stock norm (PUSTN) as a lower bound,[7] and

4. a component that allows an additional release during an emergency situation (PUSTD..EM), in which case stocks are allowed to go below the norm but not below 10% of the previous year's level of stocks.

$$PUST = MAX(0.1 * PUST(-1), MAX(PUST..EQ + PRCU..ADD, PUSTN * 0.9) - PUSTD..EM)$$

In the central baseline projections it is assumed that none of the MAX conditions in the PUST equation are triggered so that PUST..EQ = PUST. MSP and PUSTN are part of the stockholding policy variables mentioned in Figure 2.A1.

The PUST..EQ equation assumes that public stock levels are dependent on the stock norm in a country. Therefore the PUST..EQ equation is defined relative to that norm. However, the relationship changes with the level of the norm following the assumption that at higher norm levels the relation is likely to weaken.

$$LN\left(\frac{PUST..EQ}{PUSTN}\right)$$
$$= \alpha_{PUST..EQ} + \beta_{PUST..EQ,PP}\ LN\left(\frac{3 * PP}{PP(-1) + PP(-2) + PP(-3)}\right)$$
$$+ \beta_{PUST..EQ,PUSTN}\ LN(PUSTN)$$

The price ratio elasticities ($\beta_{PUST..EQ,PP}$) were generally taken from the former total stock equations in Aglink-Cosimo and average around -0.4. The elasticities $\beta_{PUST..EQ,PUSTN}$ range between -0.3 and 0 for the eight countries.

The additional procurement component reflects the assumption that the public sector buys any quantity at the guaranteed procurement prices (MSP):

$$PRCU..ADD = MAX(0, MSP * 0.9 - PP) * 100$$

The PRCU..ADD equation guarantees that additional procurement becomes completely price elastic when the market price drops below 90% of the MSP. That is, as soon as the market price is lower than 90% of the MSP, then any quantity will be procured in order to keep the price above that value. These types of equations are regularly used in Aglink-Cosimo to switch between a market that clears for prices to one that clears for a certain quantity – in this case additional procurement and implicitly total stocks. The choice of 90% of the MSP is motivated by the fact that market price support is unlikely to work perfectly and as a result it takes some time for government procurement to react to price drops.

Public stock releases

Total public stock releases (PUSTD) are a function of subsidised consumer prices (CP..SUB) relative to open market consumer prices (CP), the market price (PP) relative to its average over the past three years, the stock norm (higher norms increase distribution – but only slightly) as well as the population of a country (POP). A further restriction guarantees that the stock release is at least as big as the decrease in public stocks and that distributions do not occur if public stocks are zero. The latter is guaranteed through the last term $(1/1+e^\wedge(...))$ at the end of the PUSTD equation. This term evaluates to values close to but below 1 as long as public stocks are greater than 20 kt and evaluates to values close to but above 0 if public stocks approach 0 kt. For any volumes in between 20 kt and 0 kt, it smoothly reduces from values slightly below 1 to values slightly above 0. These types of sigmoid functions are widely used in equilibrium models to allow a variable to perform a 'step' around certain values. A classic example of this are applied tariffs which depend on the fill rate of tariff rate quotas (see equation 70 in OECD, 2015).

$$LN(PUSTD..EQ)$$
$$= \alpha_{PUSTD..EQ} + \beta_{PUSTD..EQ,CP} \, LN\left(\frac{CP..SUB}{CP}\right)$$
$$+ \beta_{PUSTD..EQ,PP} \, LN\left(\frac{3 * PP}{PP(-1) + PP(-2) + PP(-3)}\right)$$
$$+ \beta_{PUSTD..EQ,PUSTN} \, LN(PUSTN) + \beta_{PUSTD..EQ,POP} \, LN(POP)$$

The elasticity $\beta_{PUSTd..EQ,CP}$ is only relevant for countries that distribute at subsidised prices and averages around -0.1. The price ratio elasticity ($\beta_{PUSTD..EQ,PP}$) averages around 0.3 and the elasticity of the stock norm ($\beta_{PUSTD..EQ,PUSTN}$) around 0.05. The population elasticity ($\beta_{PUSTD..EQ,POP}$) was set at about 0.15.

$$PUSTD = MAX(PUSTD..EQ + PUSTD..EM, PUST(-1) - PUST) * \frac{1}{1 + e^{10(10-PUST)}}$$

Release from public stocks can occur through three channels: in the domestic market at market prices, in the domestic market at subsidised prices or in the international market at export prices. The countries in this study only use one or two of these three channels. For the countries that only have one channel of distribution, total distribution is set equal to the distribution through this channel. This means that total distribution is set equal to distribution at subsidised prices for Bangladesh and the Philippines, while total distribution is equal to distribution at domestic prices in Japan and Korea, and equal to exports in Thailand. Indonesia and India have a combination of subsidised and domestic distribution at market prices. For those two countries, the equation for subsidised distribution is exactly the same as the one for PUSTD..EQ, but elasticities are generally less reactive to price changes to ensure that subsidised release is more stable than release at market prices.

Emergency public stock releases can occur when rice availability is at risk. In the model, emergency stock releases are triggered when market prices increase above a certain threshold. This threshold is set at 5% above the reference price PP..REF, which corresponds to the price in the baseline scenario.[8] In this case, a certain amount of public stocks will be released. The parameter γ identifies how much of the beginning stocks should be available for emergency releases. It can also – when set to zero – be used to deactivate the mechanism. In the yield shock scenario γ is chosen to be quite high at 95% making almost the entire beginning stocks available for emergency releases.

$$PUSTD..EM$$
$$= PUST(-1)(1 - PUST..LOSS) * \gamma * MIN\left(1, MAX\left(0, \frac{PP}{PP..REF} - 1.05\right) * 100\right)$$

Public stock procurement

Public stock procurement (PRCU) is modelled residually: it is a function of public stocks' change (which incorporates a loss factor) and distribution.

$$PRCU = PUST - PUST(-1)(1 - PUST..LOSS) + PUSTD$$

The additional procurement variable (PRCU..ADD) and total procurement (PRCU) are linked via the public stock equation. The public stock equation explicitly contains PRCU..ADD and since total procurement is calculated as shown above, PRCU..ADD enters into PRCU as well.

As is the case with distribution, countries use not more than two of the three existing procurement channels. For those that use only one procurement channel (Japan and Korea exclusively procure in the domestic market at prevailing market prices, while India exclusively procures in the domestic market at the MSP), total procurement is set equal to procurement through that one channel. The other countries use a combination of procurement at guaranteed prices and procurement from imports. Procurements from imports (PRCU..IM) are defined as a share of total procurement. This share is defined as:

$$PRCU..IM = PRCU * MAX\left[0, \frac{\mu PP^{\delta}}{(\mu PP^{\delta} + IMP^{\delta})} - 0.01\right]$$

The exponent δ defines the substitutability between the two procurement channels and μ is used to calibrate to observed shares. For some countries, the general instrument to procure rice from international markets does exist, but is rarely used (Bangladesh, India, Indonesia, the Philippines). In those countries, PRCU..IM was assumed to be zero when building the baseline framework. In order to make it possible to calibrate the PRCU..IM equation to those specific situations with zero observations, the μ parameter is chosen so that the fraction evaluates to a value smaller than 0.01 which causes the MAX operator to evaluate to zero. This specification hence allows scenarios in which procurement from imports will kick in when the relation between the domestic price and the sum of domestic and import price becomes larger than 0.01. The choice of 0.01 is arbitrary and could benefit from further sensitivity analysis in future.

Subsidised procurement is then the residual of total procurement and those from imports.

Notes

[1] The documentation of the Aglink-Cosimo model can be consulted at http://www.agri-outlook.org/abouttheoutlook/Aglink-Cosimo-model-documentation-2015.pdf.

[2] Examples are biofuel feedstock and the crushing of oilseeds.

[3] The FAPRI model documentation is available at https://www.fapri.missouri.edu/wp-content/uploads/2015/02/FAPRI-MU-Report-09-11.pdf.

[4] Procurement on the domestic market can occur at prevailing market prices or at procurement prices, while distribution on the domestic market can occur at prevailing market prices or at subsidised prices.

[5] In general, private stocks should help mitigate price variability. However, the private stock levels are much lower than the public ones in several of the countries in this study, and therefore their variation cannot compensate that of public stocks.

6   The procurement price is modelled as a Minimum Support Price, which explains the choice for the acronym MSP.

7   Even though it initially seemed appropriate to use the norm itself as a lower bound for public stocks, historical data show that public stock levels fall below the norm from time to time. To reflect this, the lower bound in the model was set at 90% of the norm.

8   The threshold of 5% above the reference price was chosen after several trial and error simulations based on the 10% yield shock scenario. The stockholding policies of the eight countries can contain rules for emergency stock release, but usually there are no clearly defined triggers that explain when exactly emergency distribution will occur as the trigger is likely to be different depending on the situation.

Chapter 3. Medium-term market effects of alternative public stockholding policies

This chapter examines what would happen to domestic and international markets over the medium term (2018-2030) if current public stockholding policies were to remain in place (baseline scenario) compared to a situation whereby the eight selected Asian countries in this report collectively increased (high-level scenario) or decreased (low-level scenario) their public stock levels. The analysis shows that the strongest impacts would occur during the three-year transition period when countries adjust their public stocks to the new levels. It also shows there would be structural impacts over the medium term, although at a lower intensity, on procurement, domestic and international prices, availability, private stock levels, and public expenditure. In the event of a global production shock, the model projects that the immediate impact on prices and availability would be less severe under the high-level scenario, but that recovery towards the no-shock situation would be faster and public expenditure lower when countries hold smaller public stocks.

3.1. Description of scenarios

This chapter examines what would happen in domestic and international markets if all eight countries set their public stock levels to either a high or low level at the same time. The benefit of this scenario is that it establishes bounds to the global market impacts that derive from changes in public stock policies across the region. The fact that all these countries react in the same way could be the result of a period of relatively high (low) prices or price volatility. This was, for example, the case during the food price crisis in 2007-08 when several countries began to expand their public stocks in response to higher and more volatile prices.

To model these two scenarios, the norm for public stocks is adjusted to a high level (*high-level scenario*) or a low level (*low-level scenario*). Both scenarios are stylised experiments and are not designed to represent specific policies under consideration by specific countries. The level at which countries set their norms is expressed in days of national consumption. The advantage of this measure is that it allows for straightforward comparisons across countries. Furthermore, the norms of public stocks are often expressed in days of national consumption when they have a food security objective.

The level of public stock norms under the high-level scenario is set at three months of national consumption, while the level of public stock norms under the low-level scenario is set at two weeks. These values were chosen by examining public stocks over the past decades in the selected countries. The transition towards the high or low public stock norm levels is assumed to occur linearly during the three-year period 2018-2020.

Figure 3.1 shows the average public[1] stock levels and norms under the baseline as well as under the low- and high-level scenarios after the transition period. The norms under the baseline differ by country and reflect the most recent information available, whereas the norms under the high- and low-level scenarios are set uniformly across countries, namely 91 days under the high-level scenario and 14 days under the low-level scenario. In the case of the People's Republic of China (hereafter "China"), there was no historic information on public stock levels and norms. For the baseline, the norm in China was set at 52 days, which was selected because it is the midpoint between the low- and high-level scenarios.[2] In Thailand, the baseline assumes that no public stocks are held and therefore the norm is set at zero.

For all countries, the high-level scenario translates into an increase in the norm (and public stock levels) compared to the baseline. In the case of the low-level scenario, the norm and public stock levels are lower than under the baseline in all countries except two, Bangladesh and Thailand. In Bangladesh, the low-level scenario and baseline are the same. In Thailand, both the low- and high-level scenarios lead to an increase in the norm and public stock levels compared to the baseline.

The scenarios examine what happens if countries decide to change their stockholding policies by changing the norm. They assume that the functioning of the stockholding policies remains unchanged, i.e. the acquisition and distribution rules (as described in Chapter 1 and used in the Aglink-Cosimo model) stay in place. For example, a country that traditionally has not distributed rice from public stocks at a subsidised price will not start doing this under the low- and high-level scenarios. The only way a country changes its policy is by adjusting the norm. This is a common stockholding policy practice as norms are set to ensure that stock levels are sufficient to meet certain acquisition or distribution targets.

**Figure 3.1. Average public stock levels and norms under the baseline,
low-, and high-level scenarios, 2021-2030**

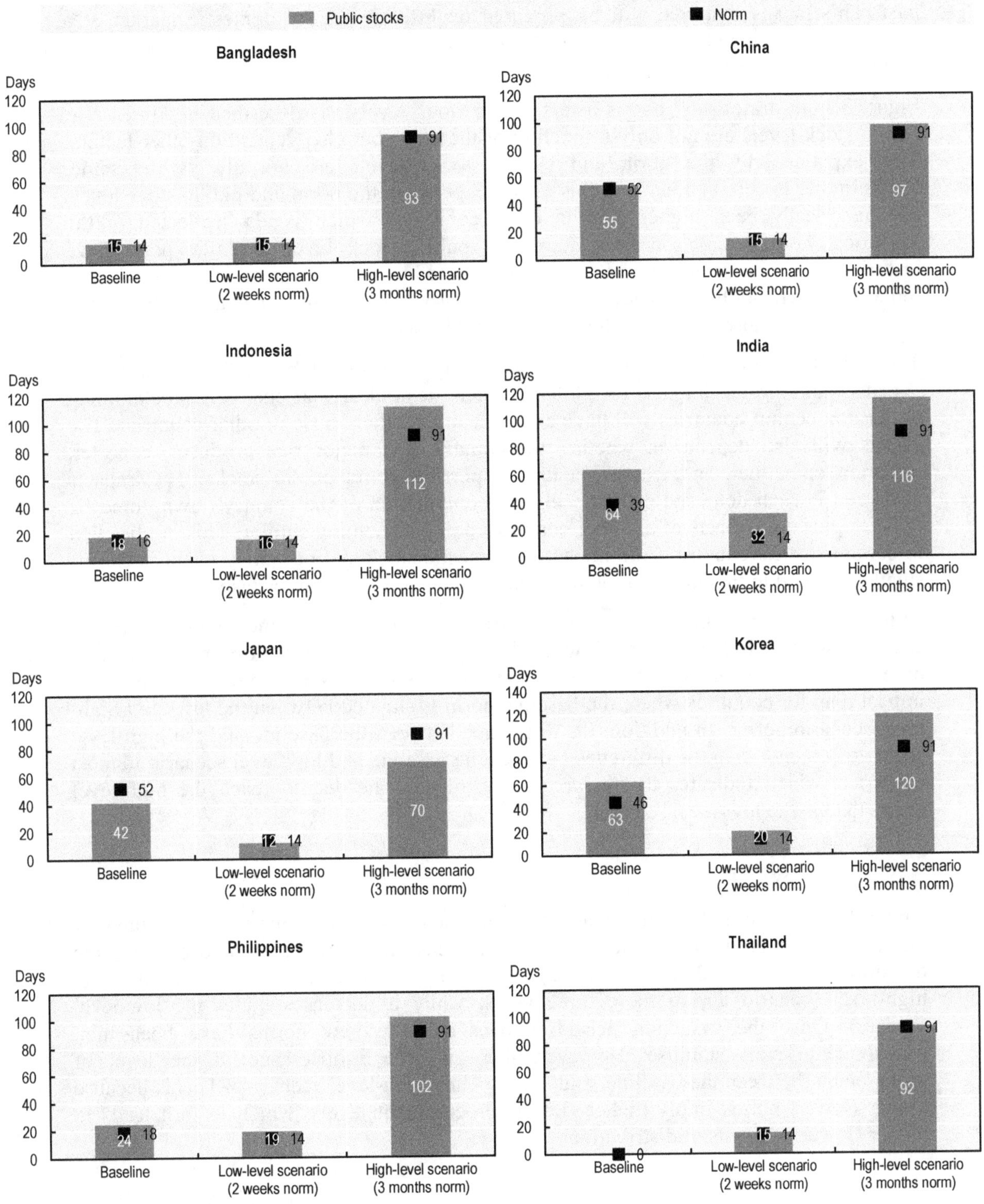

Note: Expressed in days of national consumption. Public stock data in Japan and Korea refer to public stocks composed of domestic rice.
Source: OECD simulations.

The exception to this assumption is Thailand. Under the baseline projections, there are practically no public stocks. In order to implement the low- and high-level scenarios, it was assumed that Thailand would resume the stockholding policies it had in place in the past. This means that rice will be procured exclusively on the domestic market at a procurement price and that all rice from public stocks will be exported. The procurement price was set below the market price.

Figure 3.1 illustrates how norms affect public stock levels. As described in Annex 2.A, public stock levels are not only a function of the norm but also depend on other factors. This explains why the norm and public stocks levels are not always the same. Furthermore, in certain countries, this disparity between the norm and public stock levels has historically been higher than in other countries, which is also reflected in the scenarios. For example, in Bangladesh the public stock levels and the norm have historically been at the same level, which is reflected in the baseline and the scenarios. In India, however, public stock levels have in recent years been higher than the norm, and this difference is also present in the baseline and the scenarios.

The market impacts of the two scenarios are analysed at the global and domestic levels. When examining the impacts on global markets, it is clear that changing stockholding policies in certain countries will have a greater impact than those in other countries. The effects will also depend on whether the country is a major rice producer, exporter, importer, or neither, and whether it uses imports to build public stocks. The impacts measured in each domestic market will be a combination of the country's own domestic policies plus the impacts of all other countries doing something similar. This implies that in certain smaller countries, the impact of domestic stockholding policy changes can be small compared to the impact of other countries behaving in a similar fashion.

With the exception of China, the scenarios are not symmetric. In some countries, notably Bangladesh and Indonesia, the low-level scenario is relatively close to the current baseline. For those countries, the move towards the high-level scenario has a much bigger impact than for countries where the baseline norm is situated between the low- and high-level scenario norms. In addition, the difference between the baseline and the high-level scenario is higher than the difference between the baseline and low-level scenario in most countries, which indicates that a larger adjustment is needed to reach the high-level scenario than the low-level scenario.

3.2. Impact on procurement

Under the low- and high-level scenarios, procurement levels are adjusted to meet the new norms. The change in procurement levels is projected to be most pronounced during the transition period, 2018-2020 (Figure 3.2). Aggregate procurement increases sharply in the high-level scenario during these three years, while it decreases under the low-level scenario. Once the transition period is over and the new norms have been met, procurement levels stabilise. However, there is still a difference in the level of procurement between the baseline, and the low- and high-level scenarios. This is because higher (lower) norms imply higher (lower) procurement levels, which in turn leads to higher (lower) amounts of distribution.

Figure 3.2. Aggregate procurement by all countries except China

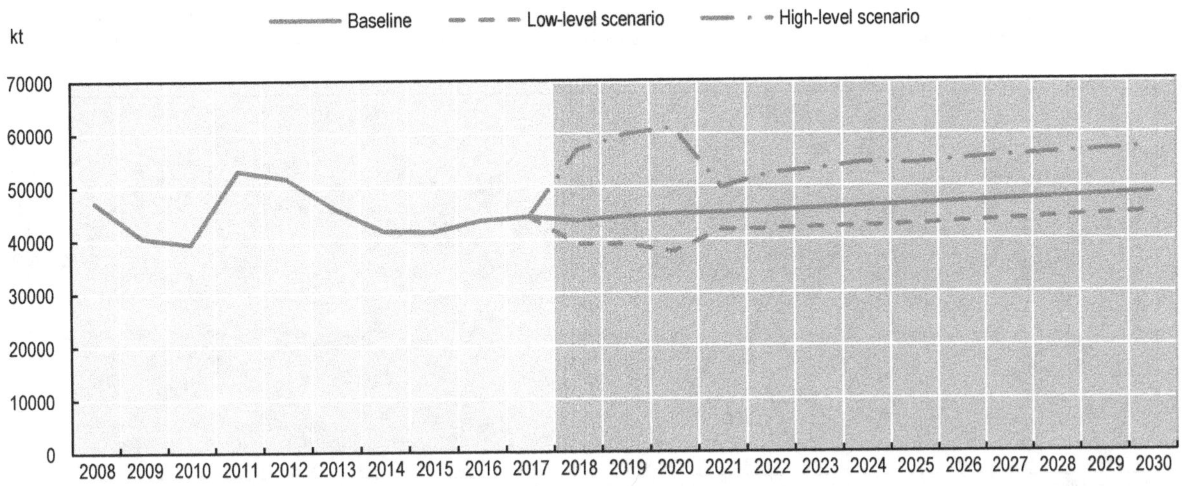

Note: China is not included in this figure because there is no information on procurement. Shaded area indicates the projection period 2018-2030.
Source: OECD simulations.

The difference in aggregate procurement between the baseline and high-level scenario is higher than the difference between the baseline and the low-level scenario. This is because the baseline norm in most countries is relatively closer to the norm in the low-level scenario than to the norm in the high-level scenario. This is also the case in India, which highly influences the aggregate procurement levels in this figure. In all three scenarios, India accounts for over 80% of aggregate procurement. However, this aggregate volume does not consider procurement in China as no information on procurement or distribution is available.

Indonesia and the Philippines regularly import rice to build public stock. For these two countries, historic information starting from 2000 is available on the volume of imports they added to their public stocks. Figure 3.3 illustrates that, historically, the volume of imports by Indonesia and the Philippines has fluctuated considerably. Over the projection period, Indonesia's procurement from imports is projected to decline slightly, following the country's overall import trend. In the Philippines, the baseline projections for public stock procurement from imports are twice as high as domestic procurement, which reflects the historical situation.

Under the high-level scenario, procurement from imports is projected to increase in both countries as the high norm cannot be reached via domestic procurement only. Under the low-level scenario, Indonesia will continue to increase its imports relative to the baseline during the transition period. As the norms of all countries are reduced under the low-level scenario, the global market is supplied with rice, which leads to a decrease in the world price. Since imports will be cheaper under the low-level scenario than under the baseline during these three years, Indonesia will increase its imports under the low-level scenario compared to the baseline. However, since the Philippines is more integrated with international markets (Furuhashi and Gay, 2017) and the price differential between the domestic and international markets is not sufficiently large, it will not increase its procurement from imports.

Figure 3.3. Procurement from imports in Indonesia and the Philippines, 2000-2030

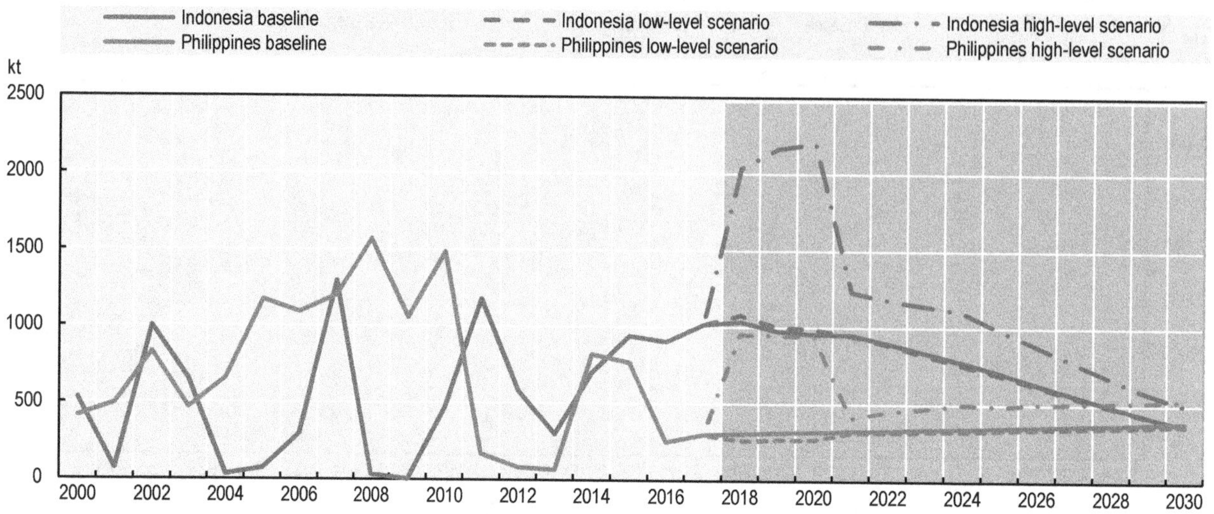

Note: Shaded area indicates the projection period 2018-2030.
Source: Historic data for Indonesia from OECD (2012) and for the Philippines from NFA (2016a, 2016b, 2017).

3.3. Impact on private stocks

An advantage of the new model is that it separates private from public stocks and incorporates the link between the two types of stock. In particular, as countries build larger public stocks, the private sector is crowded out from stockholding activities. Accordingly, the aggregate level of private stocks is higher under the low-level scenario compared to the baseline since public stocks held by all countries drops (Figure 3.4).

The impact on private stock levels is expected to be most pronounced during the transition period, when public stocks are released on the market under the low-level scenario in order to achieve their new public stock norms. During these three years, the increase in supply under the low-level scenario causes rice prices to drop in domestic markets, triggering the private sector to buy rice at low prices. In the years following the transition period, rice prices rebound and hence the private sector sells its stocks. The opposite occurs under the high-level scenario.

The level of increase or decrease in private stocks varies by country. Figure 3.5 shows the average relative change (in percentage) for each country in the level of private stocks between the baseline and the scenarios during the projection period. In all countries, except for Bangladesh, Korea and Thailand, private stocks are projected to increase in the low-level scenario relative to the baseline. In Bangladesh, the public stock levels under the low-level scenario and baseline are the same. Korea has no private stocks under the baseline and is assumed not to have private stocks under the low- and high-level scenarios. In Thailand, private stocks decrease under the low-level scenario because under the baseline Thailand does not have any public stocks (only private stocks). Hence, the move for Thailand from the baseline towards the low-level scenario implies an increase in public stocks, and thus a decrease in private stocks. Private stocks will be relatively lower for all countries under the high-level scenario compared to the baseline.

In absolute volume terms, the change in private stock levels is projected to be most pronounced in China, which is assumed to place a large share of its stocks in private storage, whereas it will be relatively small in India due to the still very large public stock levels and the limit on private stockholding.

Figure 3.4. Aggregate level of private stocks of rice

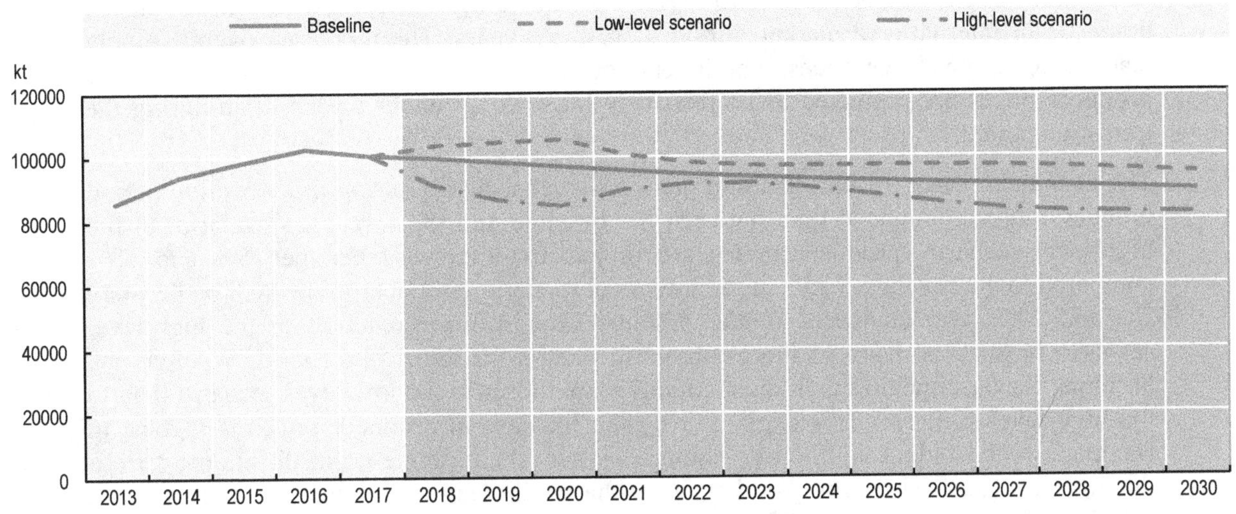

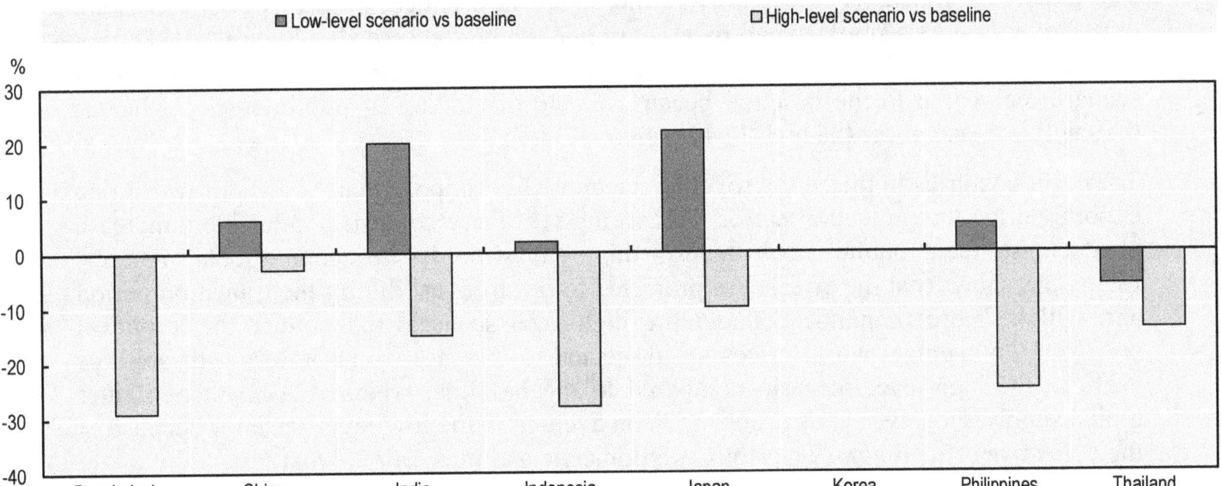

Note: Aggregate includes all eight countries in the study. Shaded area indicates the projection period 2018-2030.
Source: OECD simulations.

Figure 3.5. Average relative change in the level of private stocks between the baseline and the scenarios, 2018-2030

Source: OECD simulations.

3.4. Impact on prices

Figures 3.6 and 3.7 illustrate how producer prices in the eight countries in this study are projected to change in the low- and high-level scenarios compared to the baseline scenario. The effects, expressed in relative percentage changes, vary across the countries but are expected to be strongest during the transition period and to dissipate in the years afterwards. In the low-level scenario, rice will be released from public stocks on the domestic or international market during these three years. The increased overall supply leads to lower producer prices. The inverse occurs under the high-level scenario, where producer prices are projected to be relatively higher than under the baseline during the transition period.

The change between the baseline and the high-level scenario during the transition period is much more pronounced than between the baseline and the low-level scenario. In the high-level scenario, producer prices are projected to increase between 5% and 18% compared to the baseline, while in the low-level scenario, producer prices will be between 2% and 6% lower compared to the baseline. The stronger reaction in the high-level scenario is partly a result of the asymmetric relation of the two scenarios *vis-à-vis* the baseline: the baseline norms in most countries are closer to the low-level scenario than to the high-level scenario. This explains why the increase in producer prices is highest in Bangladesh and Indonesia, the two countries where the baseline norm differs most from the high-level scenario norm. Another factor that might lead to a higher and more volatile reaction of prices under the high-level scenario is the fact that the private sector is less involved in stockholding activities. In China, the two scenarios are modelled symmetrically, with the baseline norm at the mid-point between the low- and high-level scenarios. Still, the producer price reaction is stronger under the high-level scenario than in the low-level scenario. This suggests the role of the private sector in stabilising prices in the low-level scenario.

The impact on consumer prices mirrors the effect on producer prices as both prices are projected to follow a similar trend over the projection period (see also Figure 2.3). During the transition period consumer prices are expected to decrease under the low-level scenario compared to the baseline because of the offloading of public stocks, whereas they will increase under the high-level scenario.

The eight countries in this study together accounted for approximately 45% of world rice exports during the projection period. Accordingly, if these countries collectively increase or decrease their public stock levels, this will strongly influence global markets. Figure 3.8 shows that the effects are projected to be strongest during the transition period and will be more pronounced under the high-level scenario than under the low-level scenario. On average, world prices are projected to increase by 10% during these three years in the high-level scenario compared to the baseline, which is a result of tighter global supply. However, they drop by 4% on average in the low-level scenario because of the collective offloading of rice stocks on domestic and international markets.

Figures 3.6, 3.7 and 3.8 show that after the transition period, domestic and international prices are expected to move towards the baseline projections as farmers adjust their output in response to the price changes. That is, the relatively lower prices in the low-level scenario decrease the expected return per hectare which causes farmers to reduce their output. This in turn is projected to lead to an increase in prices in the years after the transition period. The opposite occurs under the high-level scenario, where the higher price for rice motivates farmers to produce more for the global markets during the transition period, which consecutively drives prices back down to the baseline equilibrium.

Figure 3.6. Producer prices: Percentage change in low-level scenario compared to the baseline scenario, 2017-2030

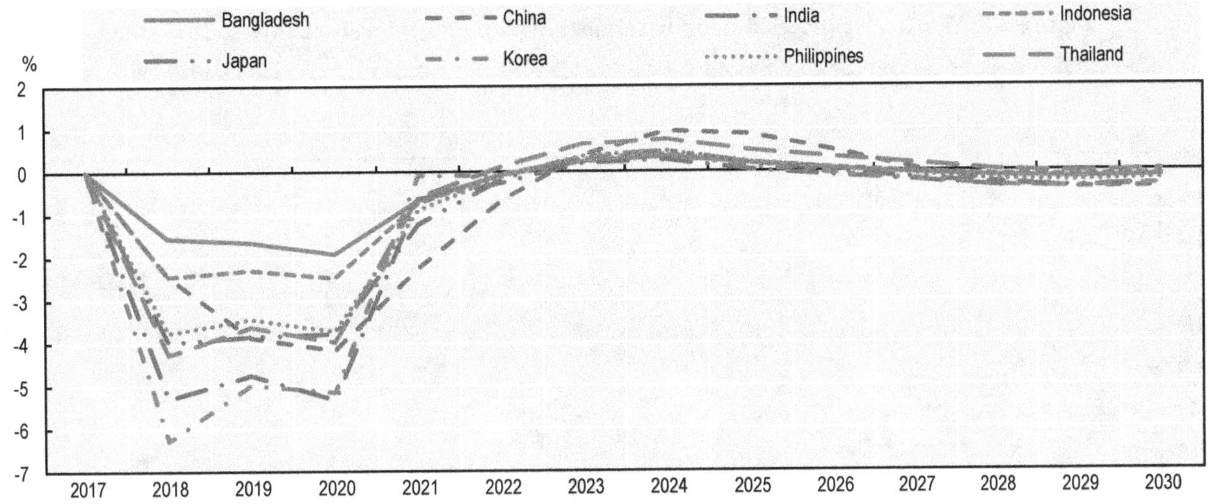

Source: OECD simulations.

Figure 3.7. Producer prices: Percentage change in high-level scenario compared to the baseline scenario, 2017-2030

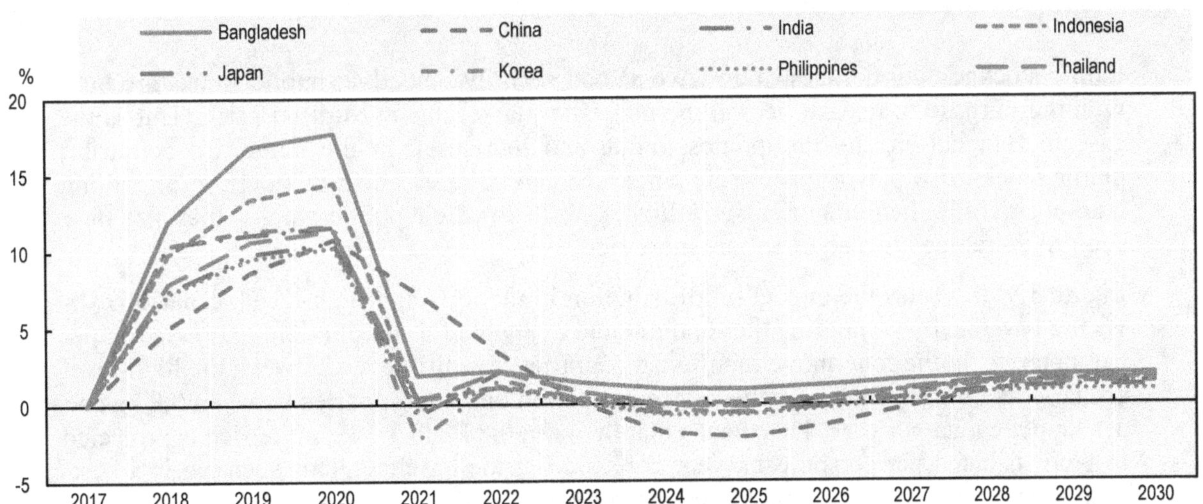

Source: OECD simulations.

Prices will not return completely to the baseline levels. Once supply has adjusted in the years following the transition period, prices under the low-level scenario are projected to consistently remain below the baseline levels while they will stay above the baseline levels under the high-level scenario. Prices are not expected to converge entirely to the baseline because procurement levels have changed under the scenarios compared to the baseline. The extent to which prices will stay above or below the baseline levels also depends on the effectiveness of the public stockholding programme. Under the current model specifications, a loss rate of 2% has been assumed for all countries, which means that average distribution levels are 2% lower than average procurement levels. However, if losses are higher, then less of the procured rice will reach markets, which will in turn induce stronger price effects, making the relative differences between the baseline, low-, and high-level scenarios more pronounced.

Figure 3.8. World rice prices during baseline, low-, and high-level scenarios, 2017-2030

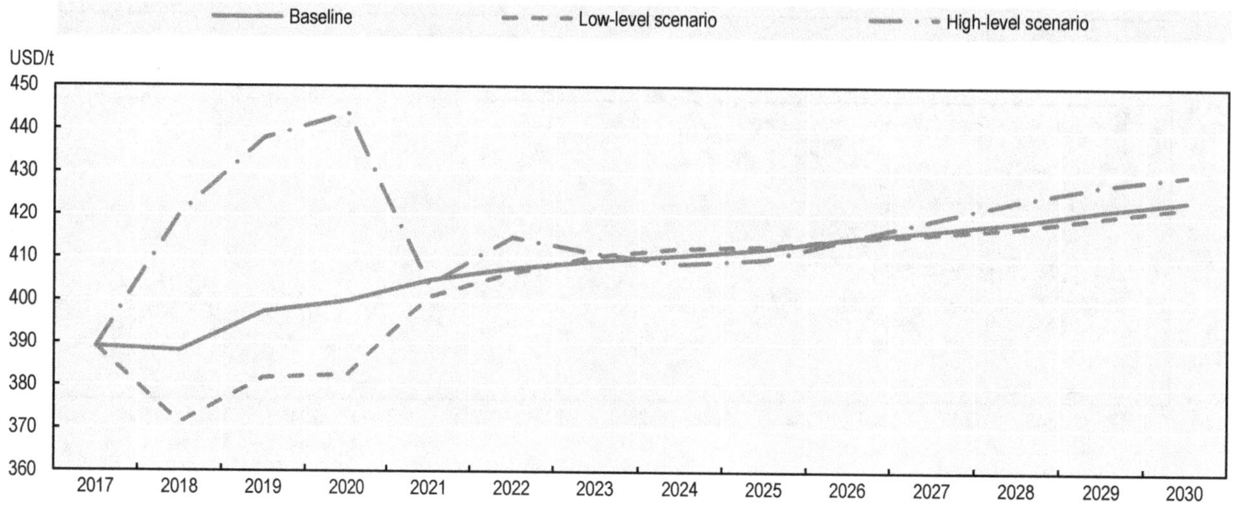

Source: OECD simulations.

3.5. Impact on availability

Public stockholding policies often have a food security objective: public stocks are built with the purpose to release rice on the domestic market at a subsidised price. This is the case in Bangladesh, the Philippines, India, and Indonesia. In the latter two countries, public stocks also play a buffer role since rice can be released from stocks at prevailing market prices. When countries set a higher norm for their public stocks, they not only acquire more rice but also distribute more rice.

Figure 3.9 illustrates the impact on distribution in the low- and high-level scenario *vis-à-vis* the baseline by comparing the total amount available for distribution, expressed in per capita terms. In the four above-mentioned countries, the difference between the high-level scenario and the baseline over the projection period on average varies between 0.8 kg and 3.1 kg per capita per year. This means that between 0.8 kg to 3.1 kg more rice is projected to be distributed per person each year compared to the baseline. This scenario is a best-case scenario as it assumes that losses are minimal (2%).

Under the low-level scenario, distribution per capita is projected to be on average less than under the baseline. The difference between the baseline and the low-level scenario is small for Bangladesh and Indonesia since for these two countries, the norm and public stock levels under the baseline and low-level scenario are the same (Bangladesh) or very close (Indonesia). In the case of India, the difference between the low-level scenario and baseline is more pronounced given the overall size of the country's public stockholding program.

Figure 3.9. Per capita distribution of rice: Average difference between the baseline, low-, and high-level scenarios, 2018-2030

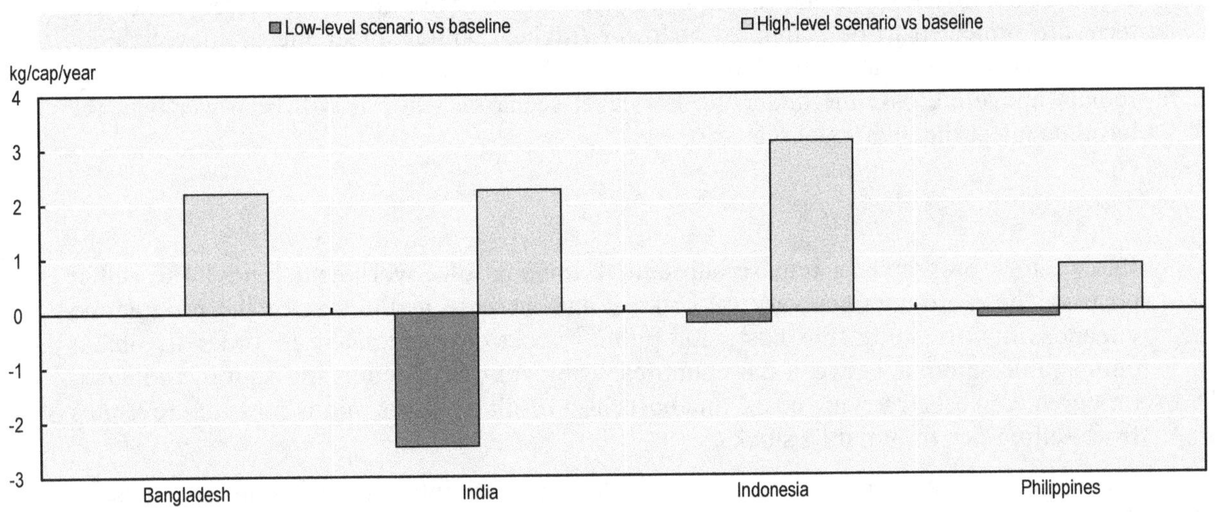

Source: OECD simulations.

Figure 3.10. Per capita rice consumption (availability): Average percentage difference between the baseline, low-, and high-level scenarios, 2018-2020 and 2021-2030

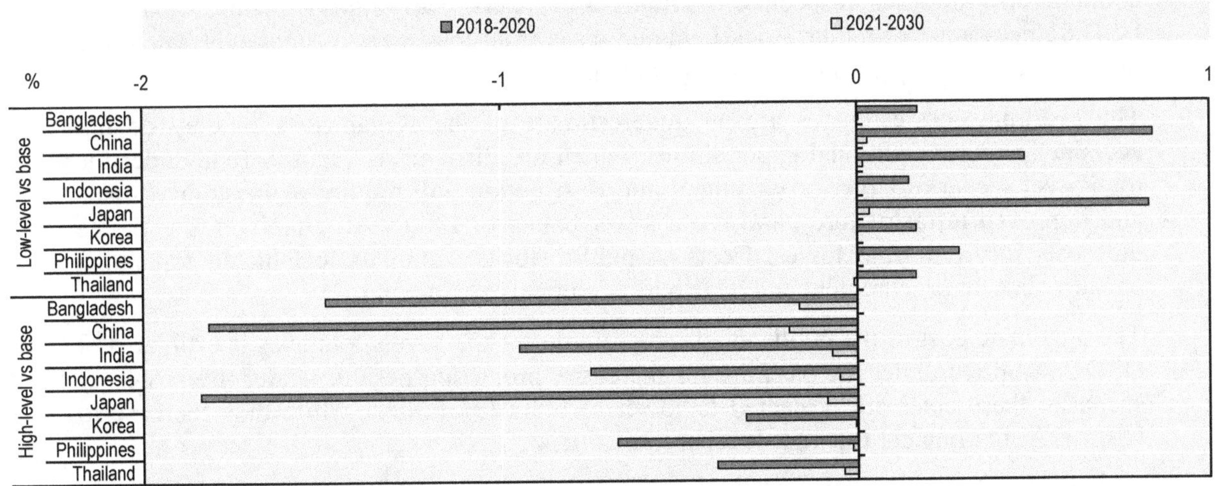

Note: Food availability is calculated based on FAO's Food Balance Sheets.
Source: OECD simulations.

Distribution of rice from public stocks is only one part of a country's overall rice availability. As indicated in the previous section, during the transition period towards the low or high-level scenario, prices are projected to decrease or increase considerably. This also affects availability. Figure 3.10 shows the relative change in per capita availability in each of the countries between the baseline and the two scenarios. A distinction is made between the transition period (2018-2020) and the post-transition period (2021-2030). During the transition period, per capita availability of rice is projected to increase under the low-level scenario compared to the baseline while it will decrease under the high-level scenario. This is a result of the offloading of rice during the transition period under the low-level scenario while under the high-level scenario more rice is procured in order to reach the high norm levels. Once the transition period is over and the new norms and public stock levels have been reached under both scenarios, per capita availability is expected to move towards the values under the baseline. Still, given that prices in the long term are projected to be stabilised at lower (higher) values under the low-level (high-level) scenario than under the baseline, availability for several countries is expected to remain above the baseline under the low-level scenario, while it will be lower than the baseline under the high-level scenario.

3.6. Impact on public expenditures

Public stock programmes require substantial amounts of government funds. The actual costs of these programmes vary by country and increase as the size of the programme expands. In this study, the costs for public stocks are estimated in order to obtain comparable amounts between the countries. They are calculated as the sum of estimated procurement costs, carrying costs, and costs as a result of losses minus potential revenues from selling rice from public stocks.

Procurement costs for each country are decomposed into the different channels of procurement. That is, procurement costs for a country that acquires rice from the domestic market at a procurement price and from imports will be decomposed into the amount procured in the domestic market times the procurement price plus the amount of rice procured in the international market times the import price. Likewise, the potential distribution revenues from selling rice from public stocks are decomposed for each country reflecting their respective distribution channels. Carrying costs are estimated at USD 84 per tonne[3] of public stock held and costs from losses are estimated at 2% of the public stocks in the previous period times the producer price.

The resulting cost estimates are an underestimate of the actual costs as they do not account for other additional expenditures, which are difficult to quantify (e.g. under the high-level scenario, larger procurement and distribution will require extra storage space and improved infrastructure), and use a lower bound of 2% for all countries to estimate the costs incurred from losses. Costs of public stocks cannot be calculated for China because data on procurement and distribution volumes are lacking.

The aggregate cost of the public stock programme for the seven countries is estimated at USD 234 billion under the baseline for the entire projection period. Under the low-level scenario, these costs are projected to lower to USD 203 billion, while they increase to USD 322 billion under the high-level scenario.

Figure 3.11 illustrates how much more (or less) countries are projected to spend on their public stockholding programme over the period 2018-2030 if they implement the high-level (or low-level) scenario. The costs are accumulated over the projection period 2018-2030 and are expressed in USD billion. In India, almost USD 39 billion more are projected to be needed to obtain and maintain the high-level scenario over this period compared to the baseline, whereas USD 26 billion can be saved by reducing the programme to the low-level scenario. Bangladesh and Indonesia are projected to spend USD 15 and USD 22 billion more, respectively, over the entire projection period if they were to implement the high-level scenario. The savings for these countries by switching to the low-level scenario are nil (Bangladesh) or minimal (Indonesia) because their baselines are the same as (Bangladesh) or very close to (Indonesia) the low-level scenario. If Thailand were to re-instate the public stockholding programme under the conditions assumed in this report (i.e. procurement price at 95% of producer price and all rice from public stocks gets exported), then the projected costs over 2018-2030 are estimated to be almost ten times more under the high-level scenario compared to the low-level scenario.

Figure 3.11. Absolute difference in cost of public stockholding programs, accumulative over projection period 2018-2030

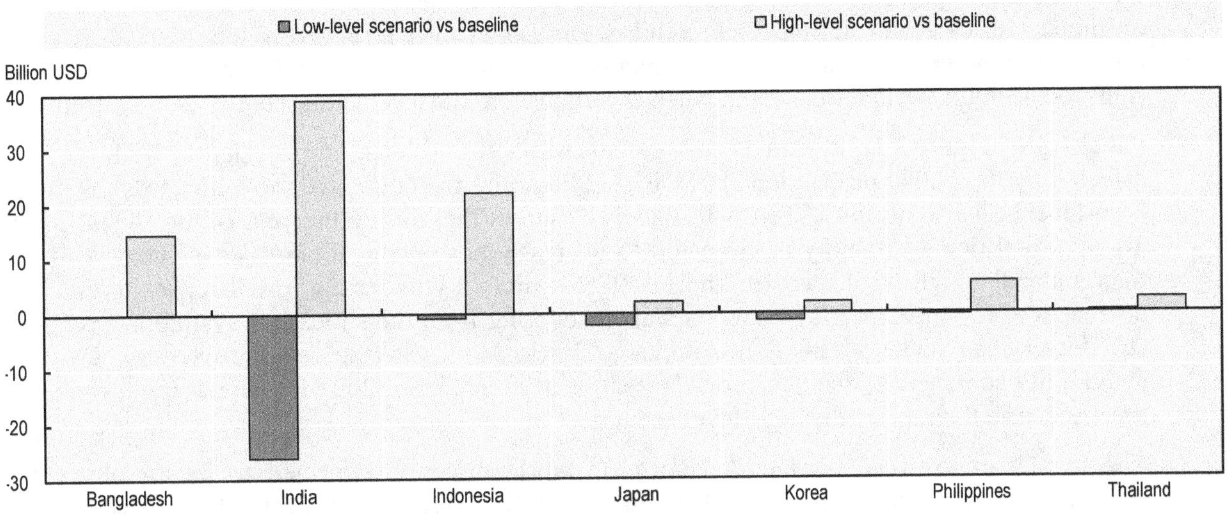

Source: OECD simulations.

3.7. Impact of a production shock

One of the main reasons why countries keep large amounts of rice in public stocks is to be prepared for emergency situations whereby domestic or global rice availability suddenly drops. In this event, they can release rice from their public stocks at either prevailing market prices or at subsidised prices. Maintaining larger public stocks of rice would provide a larger buffer against these shocks, but how much better can countries mitigate the impacts of these shocks when they keep large public stocks compared to smaller ones, and what would be the fiscal implications?

This section examines the impacts of a sudden drop in availability under the low-level scenario compared to the high-level scenario. The shock is modelled to occur in 2024. This year was chosen because by then the transitional impacts of moving towards the low- or high-level scenario will have dissipated. The shock is designed to correspond to the largest deviation from the global trend during the last 20 years: it simulates a 5% decrease in domestic production in each of the eight countries, which is equivalent to a global drop in rice production of 3%. After the shock, countries are assumed to rebuild public stocks to reach their low- or high-level scenario norm levels.

In the previous sections, one of the underlying assumptions was that the norm is used as a lower bound for the level of public stocks. Namely, it was assumed that public stocks do not go below 90% of the stock norm. However, the Aglink-Cosimo model also allows for emergency stock releases in case of a sudden drop in availability.[4] Under this emergency situation, up to 90% of available public stocks can be released. This extra specification in the model reflects the overall functioning of public stockholding programmes, whereby the level of stocks is maintained at a certain threshold under a normal price environment, but allows the release of rice under extreme circumstances.

The eight countries in this study are responsible for 75% of global rice production and 45% of global rice trade, and hence a shock in these countries will affect global rice availability and world rice prices. Figure 3.12 and Figure 3.13 illustrate the impact of a production shock on global rice availability and world rice prices, respectively. They show availability and world prices under the low- and high-level scenarios during normal times (no shock) compared to a situation with a 3% global production shock in 2024 (with shock). Figure 3.12 and Figure 3.13 are both composed of two panels. The panels on the left show the evolution of availability and prices over a relatively long period in order to put the impact of the global production shock into perspective. The panels on the right focus on the period 2024-2028 when the effects are the most prominent.

Panel (a) of Figure 3.12 illustrates that global availability of rice is projected to be less affected by the global production shock in 2024 than by the collective move towards the high-level scenario during 2018-2020. Panel (b) shows that during the year of the shock, 2024, global rice availability is projected to decrease more under the low-level scenario than under the high-level scenario and in 2025, availability under the low-level scenario decreases even more. In 2026, markets start recovering from the shock but availability is still lower than under a situation without a shock. However, the relative decrease in availability compared to the "no shock" situation is in 2026 and 2027 less under the low-level scenario than under the high-level scenario.

The impact of a global production shock on world prices is expected to be initially stronger when countries keep low public stocks, but the effects are projected to persevere for a longer period when countries keep high public stocks. Figure 3.13 illustrates that world prices in 2024 and 2025 are projected to be respectively 5% and 6 % higher under the low-level scenario if there is a shock compared to a no shock situation. Under the high-level scenario, the world price for rice in 2024 and 2025 will be almost 5% higher in the event of a shock. Panel (a) shows that these price effects are nevertheless lower than the price increase experienced during the transition period towards the high-level scenario (2018-2020). In the years following the shock, the price effects are projected to dissipate more quickly under the low-level scenario than under the high-level scenario. By 2027, the world price for rice under the low-level scenario has converged to prices under the no shock situation while it is still above the no shock situation under the high-level scenario.

Under the high-level scenario, prices take longer to come down in the event of a shock since countries are assumed to start rebuilding public stocks in the years following the shock. In 2024, public stocks are drawn down to deal with the lower availability, but once the shock is over, the stocks need to be rebuilt towards the low or high norm levels. In case of the high-level scenario, the norm is set higher and hence more rice needs to be procured in order to rebuild the stock, which in turn has a larger impact on prices and availability.

The individual countries in this study are expected to experience similar impacts on availability and prices as the global market. That is, a 3% global production shock is projected to lead to a relatively larger decrease in per capita availability and larger increase in consumer prices in 2024 and 2025 under the low-level scenario compared to the high-level scenario. In the years following the shock, prices and availability recover faster (i.e. converge faster to the no shock situation) under the low-level scenario than under the high-level scenario.

Figure 3.12. Impact of a 3% global production shock in 2024 on the global availability of rice under the low- and high-level scenarios

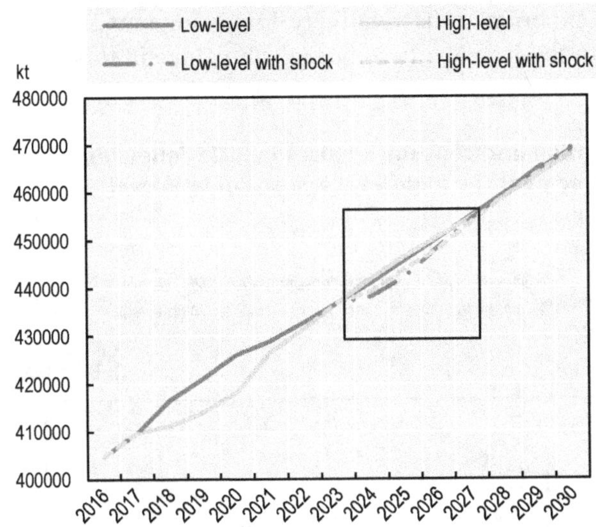

(a) Global availability under low- and high-level scenarios, without and with shock, 2016-2030

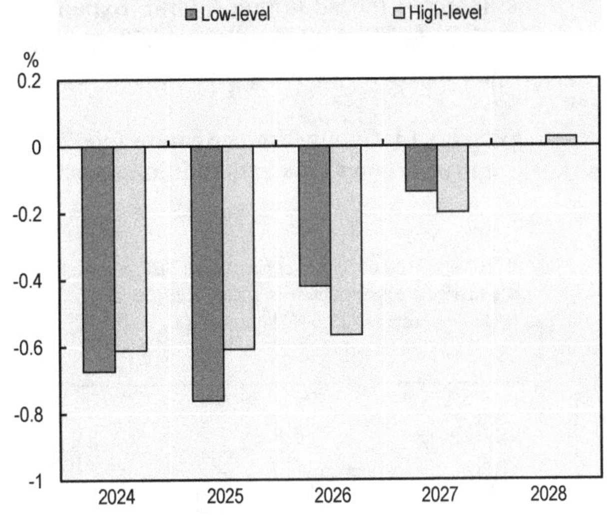

(b) % Change under low- and high-level scenarios with shock compared to a situation without shock, 2024-2028

Source: OECD simulations.

Figure 3.13. Impact of a 3% global production shock in 2024 on the world price of rice under the low- and high-level scenarios

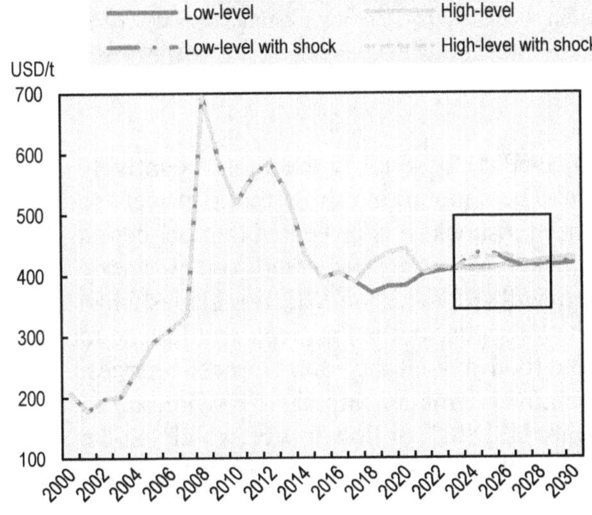

(a) Global prices under low- and high-level scenarios, without and with shock, 2016-2030

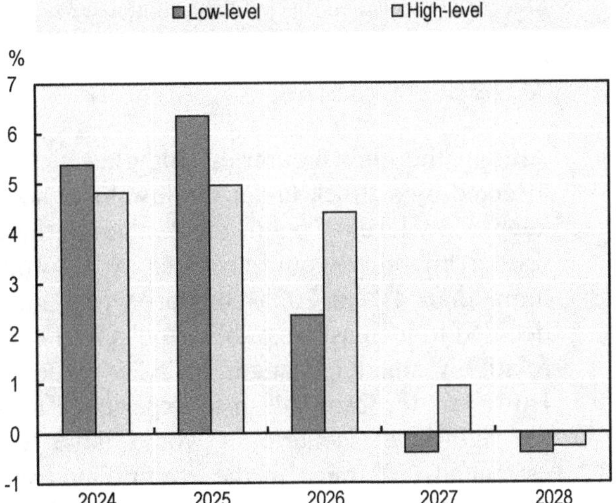

(b) % Change under low- and high-level scenarios with shock compared to a situation without shock, 2024-2028

Source: OECD simulations.

During the year of the shock, certain countries are projected to experience a stronger impact than others. Figure 3.14 shows for each country how much lower the impact of a shock is projected to be in 2025 if they had kept large public stocks versus small public stocks. The year 2025 was selected instead of 2024 because in 2025 the impact of the shock experienced under both scenarios is the strongest. Figure 3.14 also provides an estimate of the additional public expenses to experience the relatively lower impacts in 2025 under the high-level scenario compared to the low-level scenario. The values in this figure hence allow for a cost-benefit analysis.

Figure 3.14. Changes in per capita food consumption and consumer prices in 2025 following a production shock and additional costs to implement the high-level instead of low-level scenario

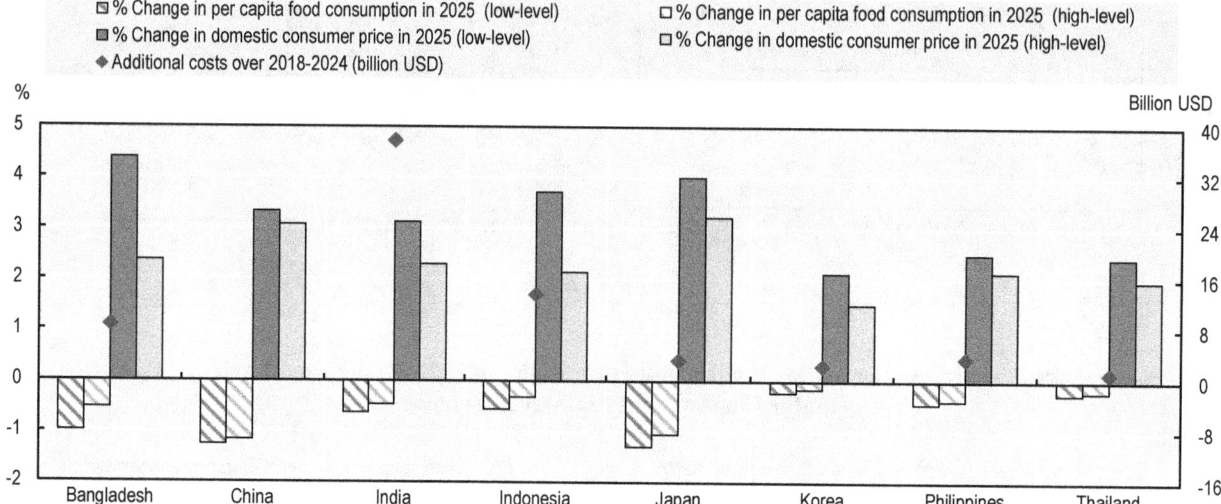

Note: The production shock refers to a global 3% production shock in 2024. Costs are estimated as described in this report. No costs could be estimated for China as there is no information on procurement and distribution volumes.
Source: OECD simulations.

Among the eight countries, Bangladesh is projected to be one of the most negatively affected by a shock under the low-level scenario. The simulations show that if it were to keep a low level of public stock, then in the event of a shock, it is projected that per capita food availability would decrease by 1% and domestic prices are projected to increase by more than 4% in 2025 compared to a situation without the shock. If Bangladesh had decided to increase its public stocks to the high-level scenario, then a shock would lead to relatively smaller changes in 2025 in per capita food availability and domestic prices. However, for Bangladesh to experience these relatively smaller impacts by switching to the high-level scenario, it would have to spend USD 8.7 billion more, which is the estimated difference in the accumulated cost of public stockholding between the high- and low-level scenarios over the period 2018-2024.

3.8. Concluding observations

Main findings

Simulations using the Aglink-Cosimo model examine what would happen over the period 2018-2030 if eight Asian countries were to collectively change their public stock levels of rice from their baseline level (*baseline*) to either a low level (*low-level scenario*) or high level (*high-level scenario*). In addition, a global drop of 3% in rice production is simulated to occur in 2024 and the relative effects of this production shock are compared under the low- and high-level scenarios.

The relative domestic impacts are projected to vary by country, but the analysis shows that there are several common trends which indicate how changing public stockholding policies can influence markets in the short and medium term.

First, the effects of changing public stockholding policies are expected to be more pronounced over the short term than over the medium term. That is, procurement levels, prices and availability will be most affected during the three-year transition period when countries adjust their public stocks to the new levels, than during the remainder of the projection period.

Under the *high-level scenario*, additional rice must be procured from domestic or international markets during the transition period, which reduces availability. This in turn leads to price increases in both the domestic and international markets. The biggest price effects are projected in Bangladesh and Indonesia, where average increases of around 14% in domestic rice prices are expected during the transition period compared to the baseline. Prices in the other six countries average between 8% and 11% above the baseline levels during those three years. But other countries are also affected as world rice prices are projected to increase by 10% compared to the baseline.

Lowering the level of public stocks, as under the *low-level scenario*, has the opposite effect. Public stocks of rice will be offloaded in the domestic or international markets, which will increase supply. During the transition period, domestic and international rice prices are projected to be on average 4% lower than under the baseline.

Second, changing public stockholding policies is expected to have structural impacts over the medium term. Whereas the effects are more pronounced during the transition period, the impacts on overall procurement, prices, availability, private stock levels, and public expenditure are expected to persist, albeit at a lower intensity, over time.

In order to reach the higher public stock norm under the *high-level scenario*, procurement must expand significantly during the transition period. However, to maintain the higher public stock level over the medium term, it will be necessary to continue to procure more rice than under the baseline. This has repercussions on the procurement channels, as domestic procurement from farmers or imports will stay at higher levels. The reverse holds under the *low-level scenario*, where lower procurement will be sustained over the entire projection period.

As relatively more rice is consistently acquired from the market in order to maintain the higher stocks under the *high-level scenario*, rice prices and availability adjust accordingly. The analysis shows that under the *high-level scenario* prices are projected to remain above the baseline levels in the medium term while availability will be lower than under the baseline. In contrast, under the *low-level scenario*, rice prices are expected to be lower and availability higher than under the baseline. The extent to which the price and availability levels differ from the baseline levels also depends in part on the effectiveness of the public stockholding programme, whereby a higher loss rate will further widen the gap between the scenario and baseline levels.

The private sector becomes crowded out from stockholding activities under the *high-level scenario* due to the increased involvement of the public sector. The level of private stocks is projected to drop under the *high-level scenario* and will stay below the baseline over the medium term. Depending on the country, the level of private stocks is projected to be 3% to 30% lower than under the baseline. In the *low-level scenario* on the other hand, the private sector will become more involved in stockholding activities, with varying levels of expansion among the countries in the study.

Expanding public stocks requires additional funds to acquire, store, manage and distribute rice. This study estimates the cost of public stocks for all the countries in the study except China. Over the next ten years, it is estimated that USD 88 billion extra would be needed to implement the *high-level scenario* in those seven countries. India would account for the majority of that amount, as it would need almost USD 39 billion more to obtain and maintain the *high-level scenario* over the period 2018-2030. A collective move towards the *low-level scenario* is projected to lead to an accumulated saving of USD 31 billion in these seven countries over the projection period.

Third, the immediate market impacts of a global production shock are projected to be less severe if countries hold larger public stocks than when they hold smaller public stocks, but recovery towards the no-shock situation is expected to occur faster when countries hold smaller public stocks. Furthermore, the higher public expenditure bill associated with the high public stocks questions whether these additional funds are not better invested in other policies that safeguard consumers from sudden supply shortages.

Policy implications

The main policy implications of this study are that countries considering changing their public stockholding programmes should take into account that the resulting impacts will not be limited to their domestic markets nor to the short term. Instead, the analysis has shown that upscaling these programmes can be costly and that changes to these programmes can structurally affect domestic markets and can have international spill-overs over the medium term.

A principal motivation that governments claim for keeping large public stocks is that these can act as a safeguard against sudden supply shocks. However, the present analysis has demonstrated that although keeping higher levels of public stocks might initially lessen the impact on price and availability from a global shock, keeping low levels of public stocks enables faster recovery towards the no-shock situation. In addition, keeping low levels of public stocks considerably reduces the burden on public finances, which frees up funds that can be used for other mitigation strategies to deal with (emergency) food shortages.

Notes

[1] Public stocks in Japan and Korea refer to public stocks composed of domestic rice.

[2] An additional set of scenarios was run with higher public stock levels (set at 50% of total stocks) and higher norms (3, 4.5, and 6 months under baseline, low-, and high-level scenarios, respectively) for China. Under the new specifications, the impacts were slightly higher in China but less pronounced in the other countries and in global markets. Given these results, the original analysis is maintained for this study in order to preserve the harmonised set-up across all countries. A future study could focus on China and examine how varying norms and public stock levels in China could affect domestic and international markets. A crucial part of such a study would be to incorporate information on the amount of rice procured at support prices and through imports, as well as information on distribution levels.

[3] The annual cost of storage per tonne of rice is based on the carrying costs of wheat and rice in India, which were USD 84 per tonne (INR 566 per quintal) in 2016-17 (Food Corporation of India, 2017). Since no information on carrying costs could be found for other countries, these costs were applied to all countries.

[4] See Annex 2.A. for the stock equations which describe these mechanisms.

References

Food Corporation of India (2017), "Accounting Year-Wise Opening Stock Adjusted Weighted Economic Cost and Acquisition Cost", available at: http://fci.gov.in/finances.php?view=23.

Furuhashi, G. and H. Gay (2017), "Market implications of the integration scenario of Southeast Asian rice markets", *OECD Food, Agriculture and Fisheries Papers*, No. 108, OECD Publishing, Paris. http://dx.doi.org/10.1787/c81e00c6-en.

NFA (2017) NFA Palay Procurement 2011-2016, available at: http://nfa.gov.ph/images/files/statistics/palayprocurement.pdf.

NFA (2016a) NFA Palay Procurement 2006-2014, available at: http://nfa.gov.ph/files/statistics/palayprocurement06-14.pdf.

NFA (2016b) Summary of NFA Rice Import Arrivals 2000-2012, available at: http://nfa.gov.ph/files/statistics/summary.pdf.

OECD (2012), *OECD Review of Agricultural Policies: Indonesia 2012*, OECD Publishing, Paris, http://dx.doi.org/10.1787/9789264179011-en.

ORGANISATION FOR ECONOMIC CO-OPERATION AND DEVELOPMENT

The OECD is a unique forum where governments work together to address the economic, social and environmental challenges of globalisation. The OECD is also at the forefront of efforts to understand and to help governments respond to new developments and concerns, such as corporate governance, the information economy and the challenges of an ageing population. The Organisation provides a setting where governments can compare policy experiences, seek answers to common problems, identify good practice and work to co-ordinate domestic and international policies.

The OECD member countries are: Australia, Austria, Belgium, Canada, Chile, the Czech Republic, Denmark, Estonia, Finland, France, Germany, Greece, Hungary, Iceland, Ireland, Israel, Italy, Japan, Korea, Latvia, Lithuania, Luxembourg, Mexico, the Netherlands, New Zealand, Norway, Poland, Portugal, the Slovak Republic, Slovenia, Spain, Sweden, Switzerland, Turkey, the United Kingdom and the United States. The European Union takes part in the work of the OECD.

OECD Publishing disseminates widely the results of the Organisation's statistics gathering and research on economic, social and environmental issues, as well as the conventions, guidelines and standards agreed by its members.

OECD PUBLISHING, 2, rue André-Pascal, 75775 PARIS CEDEX 16
(51 2018 07 1 P) ISBN 978-92-64-30535-9 – 2018